STUDYING THE HOLY
SCRIPTURES

PAUL DAVID WASHER

"Dr. Martyn Lloyd-Jones once said, 'The man whose doctrine is shaky will be shaky in his whole life.' A believer without a solid doctrinal foundation will be at the mercy of every wind of doctrine, and his usefulness in the kingdom of God will be severely limited. Hence the enormous importance of this work. Paul Washer has written a simple doctrinal compendium without being simplistic; it is deeply rooted in Scripture and presented in a memorable way. It is the book that I would like to put in the hands of every new believer in our church."

— Sugel Michelén, Pastor of **Iglesia Bíblica del Señor Jesucristo,** Author of *From and Before God*

"The Psalmist asks: 'How can a young man keep his way pure? By keeping it according to Your word.' The study of the Scriptures is a vital requirement for spiritual health and growth. Paul Washer has produced a clear, simple resource that, if followed, will help establish a young believer in his way. Especially do I appreciate Paul's emphasis on doctrine's essentiality to the Christian and to growth in the Christian life. May God give this work much usefulness!"

— Samuel Waldron, President of **Covenant Baptist Theological Seminary,** Author of *To Be Continued?*

"Secularists and pagans have always understood the importance of indoctrination at the elementary stages of instruction; but biblical Christians in our generation seem to be embarrassed by the notion, due to its association with propaganda. It is essentially, however, the mastery of information before it is critically analyzed—like the time-tested efficacy of the catechism in the history of the Church. This is done in every discipline at the basic levels, whether it is mathematics, language, science, or history. Why not the Holy Bible? The Church will lose the war in the competition of ideas in our generation if serious efforts, like this timely workbook, are not welcomed and utilized with discipline."

— Hensworth W. C. Jonas, Pastor, Executive Director of **East Caribbean Baptist Mission**

STUDYING THE HOLY **SCRIPTURES**

Published by:

HeartCry Missionary Society
PO Box 3506
Radford, VA 24143

www.heartcrymissionary.com

Printed in the United States of America 2020
First Edition

Unless otherwise noted, all Scripture quotations taken from the
New American Standard Bible® [1995]
Copyright 1960, 1962, 1963, 1968, 1971, 1972, 1973, 1975, 1977, 1995
by the Lockman Foundation. Used by permission.

Edited by Meghan Nash, Mary Claire Castleberry, and Forrest Hite
Layout and design by Mary Claire Castleberry, Michael Reece, and Forrest Hite

STUDYING THE HOLY SCRIPTURES

Table of Contents

Introduction

METHOD OF STUDY

The great goal of this study is for the student to have an encounter with God through His Word. Founded upon the conviction that the Scriptures are the inspired and infallible Word of God, this study has been designed in such a way that it is literally impossible for the student to advance without an open Bible before him or her. The goal is to help the reader obey the exhortation of the Apostle Paul in II Timothy 2:15:

> *"Be diligent to present yourself approved to God as a workman who does not need to be ashamed, accurately handling the word of truth."*

Each chapter deals with a specific aspect of Christian doctrine, divine revelation, or God's Word—the Bible. The student will complete each chapter by answering the questions and following the instructions according to the Scriptures given. The student is encouraged to meditate upon each text and write his or her thoughts. The benefit gained from this study will depend upon the student's investment. If the student answers the questions thoughtlessly, merely copying the text without seeking to understand its meaning, this book will be of very little help.

Studying the Holy Scriptures is primarily a biblical study and does not contain much in the way of colorful illustrations, quaint stories, or theological treatises. It was the desire of the author to provide a work that simply points the way to the Scriptures and allows the Word of God to speak for itself.

This workbook may be used by an individual, in a small group, for a Sunday school class, or in other contexts. It is highly recommended that the student complete each chapter on his or her own before meeting for discussion and questions with a group or discipleship leader.

EXHORTATION TO THE STUDENT

The student is encouraged to study biblical doctrine and discover its exalted place in the Christian life. The true Christian cannot bear or even survive a divorce between the emotions and the intellect or between devotion to God and the doctrine of God. According to the Scriptures, neither our emotions nor our experiences provide an adequate foundation for the Christian life. Only the truths of Scripture, understood with the mind and communicated through doctrine, can provide that sure foundation upon which we should establish our beliefs and our behavior and determine the validity of our emotions and experiences. The mind is not the enemy of the heart, and doctrine is not an obstacle to devotion. The two are indispensable and should be inseparable. The Scriptures command us to love the Lord our God with all our heart, with all our soul, and with all our mind (Matthew 22:37) and to worship God both in spirit and in truth (John 4:24).

The study of doctrine is both an intellectual and devotional discipline. It is a passionate search for God that should always lead the student to greater personal transformation, obedience, and heartfelt worship. Therefore, the student should be on guard against the great error of seeking only impersonal knowledge instead of the person of God. Neither mindless devotion nor mere intellectual pursuits are profitable, for in either case, God is lost.

THE NEW AMERICAN STANDARD BIBLE

The New American Standard Bible (1995 edition) is required to complete this study. This version of Scripture was chosen for the following reasons: (1) the unwavering conviction of its translators that the Bible is the infallible Word of God; and (2) its faithfulness to the original languages.

A WORD FROM THE AUTHOR

The Scriptures are the greatest treasure that a person can possess. They are the only source of inspired, inerrant, and infallible revelation regarding God, His will, and His works—especially His work of redemption through Jesus Christ. The Christian cannot hold too high a view of the Bible or exalt it beyond what it deserves. For these reasons and many others, the Christian should consider the study of the Scriptures to be his or her primary and lifelong task. This workbook was designed and written with these things in mind. As the student works through the material, he or she will discover why and how the Scriptures should be studied and obeyed.

I would like to thank my wife Charo for her constant support and my four children (Ian, Evan, Rowan, and Bronwyn), who continue to be a great delight. I would also like to thank HeartCry staff member Forrest Hite for his diligent and meticulous editing of the several different manuscripts that he has received. His contributions to the arrangement and overall readability of this work are as significant as they are appreciated. My thanks also are extended to the entire staff at HeartCry, who have been a great encouragement throughout the process of this book's publication.

RECOMMENDED RESOURCES FOR FURTHER STUDIES

Profiting from the Word by Arthur W. Pink
The Scripture Cannot Be Broken by John MacArthur
The Implications of Inerrancy for the Global Church by multiple authors
Can I Trust the Bible? by R. C. Sproul
40 Questions About Interpreting the Bible by Robert L. Plummer
Scripture Alone by James R. White
The Bible: God's Inerrant Word by Derek W. H. Thomas
The Canon of Scripture by Samuel Waldron
The Canon of Scripture by F. F. Bruce
The Question of Canon by Michael J. Kruger
The Inspiration and Authority of the Bible by Benjamin B. Warfield (for advanced students)
The Doctrine of the Word of God by John M. Frame (for advanced students)

ADDITIONAL NOTE

You may have noticed that this book is being sold at a strange price. Here's why: one dollar ($) from every copy sold will go directly to fund mission work through HeartCry Missionary Society (heartcrymissionary.com). The rest of the sale price is just enough to cover the cost of printing, publication, and distribution. The author is not profiting from the sale of this book, nor has he profited from the sale of any other book. Over the years, we have utilized and explored many avenues in order to publish these workbooks. Ultimately, we have reached the conclusion that doing so in-house at a low cost, even with slightly lower quality, is the most effective way of getting these useful tools into the hands of as many people across the globe as possible. We hope and pray that the Lord continues to use these books to point His people to His Word unto the edification of His Church.

Optional Study Schedule

Week One: Christian Doctrine, Part 1

Day 1: Chapter 1
Day 2: Chapter 2
Day 3: Chapter 3, Section 1
Day 4: Chapter 3, Section 2
Day 5: Read Psalm 119:1-88

Week Two: Christian Doctrine, Part 2

Day 1: Chapter 4, Section 1
Day 2: Chapter 4, Section 2
Day 3: Chapter 5, Section 1
Day 4: Chapter 5, Section 2
Day 5: Read Psalm 119:89-176

Week Three: Divine Revelation and the Trustworthiness of the Bible

Day 1: Chapter 6
Day 2: Chapter 7, Section 1, Subsections 1-2
Day 3: Chapter 7, Section 1, Subsections 3-4
Chapter 7, Section 2
Day 4: Chapter 8
Day 5: Chapter 9

Week Four: The History and Purpose of the Bible

Day 1: Chapter 10
Day 2: Chapter 11
Day 3: Chapter 12, Sections 1-2
Day 4: Chapter 12, Sections 3-4
Chapter 13, Section 1
Day 5: Chapter 13, Section 2

Week Five: The Power of God's Word

Day 1: Chapter 14
Day 2: Chapter 15, Section 1
Day 3: Chapter 15, Section 2
Day 4: Chapter 16, Section 1
Day 5: Chapter 16, Section 2

Week Six: The Believer's Response to the Scriptures, Part 1

Day 1: Chapter 17, Section 1
Day 2: Chapter 17, Section 2
Day 3: Chapter 18
Day 4: Chapter 19
Day 5: Chapter 20

STUDYING THE HOLY SCRIPTURES

Week Seven: The Believer's Response to the Scriptures, Part 2

PART ONE

AN INTRODUCTION TO CHRISTIAN DOCTRINE

Chapter 1: Christian Doctrine

In this chapter, we will define the term "Christian doctrine" and consider its great importance in the life of every believer.

CHRISTIAN DOCTRINE DEFINED

Many Christians are intimidated by the term "doctrine." They believe that the subject is too high or difficult for the common Christian and should be reserved for the professional theologian or scholar. In this study, we will learn that this attitude toward doctrine is unbiblical and unhealthy. Christian doctrine can and should be studied and understood by all. To begin our journey into this marvelous theme, we will learn concise definitions of the terms "doctrine" and "Christian doctrine."

> **Doctrine:** The word literally means, "teaching." In the Old Testament, the word is derived from the Hebrew word **lekah**, which means, "what is received" (Deuteronomy 32:2; Job 11:4; Proverbs 4:2; Isaiah 29:24). In the New Testament, the word is derived from the Greek word **didaskalía**, which refers to "the act of teaching" (I Timothy 4:13, 16; 5:17; II Timothy 3:10, 16) or "what is taught" (Matthew 15:9; II Timothy 4:3).

> **Christian Doctrine:** The beliefs that are held, practiced, and taught by Christians and are formed from a systematic study of the Old and New Testament Scriptures.

Christian doctrine is simply **the teachings of the Bible that we as Christians believe, practice, and teach to others**. If you have studied the Bible, then you have studied doctrine. If at one time you have shared what you have learned with others, then you have taught doctrine. Therefore, in one way or another, every Christian is a theologian!

1. According to the above teaching, how is "Christian doctrine" defined? Fill in the blanks.

   a. *The B_____ that are H_____, P_____,*

   and T_____ by Christians and are F_____ from a

   S_____ study of the O_____ and N_____ Testament Scriptures.

2. Based on the truths we have considered, write a definition of "Christian doctrine" in your own words.

   _____

   _____

_____

_____

_____

_____

3. Based on the truths we have considered, is the study of doctrine only for professional theologians, or is it for all Christians? Explain your answer.

_____

_____

_____

_____

_____

_____

_____

_____

THE MAJOR THEMES OF CHRISTIAN DOCTRINE

The word "doctrine" encompasses everything that the Bible teaches. For this reason, it is helpful to organize biblical doctrine into different categories. In this section of our study, we will follow the classical outline, organizing the great doctrines of the Bible into sixteen different categories.

Bibliology (Greek: *biblía* = books + *logía* = study or discourse): The study of the Bible. It encompasses divine revelation, the formation of the Scriptures, and the Bible's authority and use in the Christian life. It may also include hermeneutics (Greek: *hermēneúō* = to interpret), which is the study of the principles of Bible interpretation.

Theology (Greek: *theós* = God + *logía* = study or discourse): The study of God. It encompasses the nature, attributes, and works of God. The term is also used in reference to the study of all doctrine.

Christology (Greek: *Christós* = Christ + *logía* = study or discourse): The study of Christ. It encompasses Christ's nature and works, especially His life, death, resurrection, and glorification.

Pneumatology (Greek: *pneúma* = spirit + *logía* = study or discourse): The study of the Holy Spirit. It encompasses His nature and works, especially with regard to conversion and the Christian life.

Angelology (Greek: *ággelos* or *ángelos* = angel + *logía* = study or discourse): The study of angels. It encompasses the nature and ministry of angels as servants of God.

Demonology (Greek: *dáimōn* = demon + *logía* = study or discourse): The study of demons. It encompasses the nature, works, and final judgment of Satan and demons.

Anthropology (Greek: *ánthrōpos* = man + *logía* = study or discourse): The study of man. It encompasses the creation, fall, nature, and need of man.

Soteriology (Greek: *sōtêrion* = salvation + *logía* = study or discourse): The study of salvation. It encompasses the cross and resurrection of Christ; the sovereignty of God and man's responsibility; repentance, faith, and works; and the justification, assurance, sanctification, and final glorification of the believer.

Ecclesiology (Greek: *ekklēsía* = church + *logía* = study or discourse): The study of the Church. It encompasses the Church's foundation, purpose, organization, ordinances, and responsibilities.

Eschatology (Greek: *éschatos* = last [things] + *logía* = study or discourse): The study of the last days. It encompasses death, heaven and hell, the second coming of Christ, and the final destiny of creation.

Ethics (Greek: *ēthikós* from *êthos* = custom, moral habit): The study of moral values. It addresses the proper worldview and behavior of the Christian with respect to human life and morality.

Devotional Life: The study of the devotional disciplines as they are set forth in the Scriptures and practiced throughout the history of the Church. It encompasses such disciplines as the study of Scripture, prayer, fasting, confession, meditation, and worship.

Christian Ministry: The study of spiritual gifts and the various ministries in the local church, with a special emphasis given to pastoral ministry and proclamation.

Evangelism (Greek: *euaggélion* or *euangélion* = good news): The study of the specific content of the gospel and how to communicate it biblically to others.

Missiology (Latin: *missio* = to send, send out + Greek: *logía* = study or discourse): The study of the missionary work of the Church. It encompasses the Great Commission, the individual missionary call, the spiritual needs of the world, and the biblical methodology of missions.

Counseling: The study of biblical counseling with a view to the spiritual, intellectual, and emotional needs of individuals.

1. Review the major themes of doctrine in the previous two pages until you have committed them to memory. Then match each term with its proper definition.

_____ Bibliology

_____ Theology

_____ Christology

_____ Pneumatology

_____ Angelology

_____ Demonology

_____ Anthropology

_____ Soteriology

_____ Ecclesiology

_____ Eschatology

_____ Ethics

_____ Devotional Life

_____ Christian Ministry

_____ Evangelism

_____ Missiology

_____ Counseling

a. The study of the person and work of the Holy Spirit.

b. The study of the use of Scripture for counseling.

c. The study of God's work of salvation.

d. The study of the purpose, organization, and ordinances of the Church.

e. The study of the content of the gospel and how to communicate it biblically to others.

f. The study of moral values as set forth in the Scriptures.

g. The study of the formation, authority, and use of the Scriptures.

h. The study of the devotional disciplines as set forth in the Scriptures and practiced in Church history.

i. The study of the creation, fall, nature, and need of man.

j. The study of the nature, works, and final destiny of Satan and demons.

k. The study of the Great Commission and the missionary work of the Church.

l. The study of the person and work of Jesus Christ.

m. The study of the nature and ministry of angels.

n. The study of ministry in the local church with a special emphasis on pastoring and proclamation.

o. The study of the nature, attributes, and works of God.

p. The study of the last days, the second coming of Christ, and the final destiny of creation.

Chapter 2: The Source of Christian Doctrine

For our doctrine to be correct, it must be derived from an authoritative source—one that speaks without error regarding God, His works, and His plan for us. In the entire world, there is only one source of divine knowledge with such credentials—the Bible. One of the most crucial truths that we will learn in this study is that the Bible is the only absolute authority for our beliefs, practices, and teaching. All of our doctrine must be derived from the Holy Scriptures.

1. Based upon the teaching of the Apostle Paul in II Timothy 3:16, explain why the Bible is the only worthy and authoritative source of Christian doctrine.

_____

_____

_____

_____

_____

NOTES: The word "inspired" comes from the Greek word **theópneustos**, which may be literally translated, "God-breathed." The fact that the Bible is the inspired and infallible Word of God carries great meaning for the Christian. Its teaching is absolutely trustworthy, its promises are always faithful, and its commands and principles are the very wisdom of God. The wise can establish their doctrine and build their lives upon the Scriptures.

2. The Bible is the only absolute authority for Christian doctrine. Nevertheless, many commit the error of building their belief systems and practices upon unbiblical and untrustworthy sources. Identify these sources below according to their respective texts.

_____ *Jeremiah 17:9*   a. *Religious or mystical experiences (angelic messages, visions, etc.).*

_____ *Proverbs 14:12*   b. *The human heart.*

_____ *Matthew 15:6-9*   c. *The philosophies, traditions, and principles of the world.*

_____ *Colossians 2:8*   d. *The ways, thoughts, and opinions of men.*

_____ *Colossians 2:18*   e. *The traditions and precepts of men.*

NOTES: It is of greatest importance that we hold to the conviction that the Bible is the only absolute authority from which to derive our doctrines, beliefs, and practices. The human heart is deceitful, the intellect can be mistaken, the traditions of men can be contrary to Scripture, and religious experiences such as visions and dreams can be deceptive. An excellent rule to follow is to compare everything that we think, feel, see, and hear to the Word of God. That which does not agree with the Scriptures should be rejected.

3. Knowing that the Bible is the only infallible source and authority for all Christian doctrine, how should the Christian respond? What do the following texts from the Old and New Testaments teach us?

   a. *Joshua 1:8*

   _____

   _____

   _____

   _____

   b. *Psalm 119:105*

   _____

   _____

   _____

   _____

   c. *Matthew 4:4*

   _____

   _____

_____

_____

_____

d. *Matthew 7:24-27*

_____

_____

_____

_____

e. *II Timothy 2:15*

_____

_____

_____

_____

f. *Colossians 3:16*

_____

_____

_____

_____

4. Describe your relationship with the Bible. Does the Bible have an important place in your daily life? Is the Bible the foundation of all your beliefs and practices? Is there a need for you to make some changes in your priorities?

_____

_____

_____

_____

_____

_____

_____

_____

_____

Chapter 3: The Importance of Christian Doctrine

Part One: Doctrine and Christianity

The great majority of Christians oftentimes neglect the study of Christian doctrine. The following excuses for this neglect are often heard:

> **Objection 1:** "The Christian needs Jesus, not doctrine."
>
> **Objection 2:** "Christianity is a religion of the heart and not the intellect."
>
> **Objection 3:** "Doctrine quenches Christian zeal."
>
> **Objection 4:** "Doctrine is not practical and has little use in the Christian life."
>
> **Objection 5:** "Doctrine causes division."
>
> **Objection 6:** "Doctrine is too difficult for the common Christian."

Even though these objections are very popular within contemporary Christianity, they are unsound and demonstrate an ignorance of biblical Christianity and the will of God as it is revealed in the Scriptures. In this chapter and the two that follow, we will refute these objections one-by-one and demonstrate the vital importance of biblical doctrine in the Christian life.

THE CHRISTIAN NEEDS JESUS AND DOCTRINE

In every way, Jesus is all we need for salvation. However, how can we recognize the real Jesus without any knowledge of biblical doctrine? The Bible teaches that there will be false Christs who will attempt to deceive us, and we know that even many of the most recognizable cults claim to believe and preach Jesus. How can we be sure that we have believed in the true Christ if we have not studied the Scriptures and formed a biblical doctrine of His person and works? Furthermore, how can we be sure that we are living according to His will if we have not studied His teachings that have been revealed to us through the Scriptures? We must recognize that doctrine is indispensable if we are to believe and live correctly before God and men.

1. According to Matthew 7:28-29, what did the crowds admire?

_____

_____

_____

NOTES: It is notable that the word "teaching" comes from the Greek word ***didachê***, which can also be translated, "instruction" or "doctrine" (KJV). The Lord Jesus Christ was the best of all teachers. He knew and understood the essentiality of doctrine and taught it frequently to His disciples and the multitudes that gathered to hear His words. Humanity's greatest need is to know God and to understand His will. Jesus came to reveal God to men and to show them His will through the practice of His life and the words of His teaching.

2. In Mark 4:24-25, what warning did Jesus give to His disciples regarding His teaching (doctrine) and their responsibility to value, comprehend, and persevere in it?

   _____

   _____

   _____

   _____

NOTES: The phrase "take care" is translated from the Greek word ***blépō***, which literally means, "look" or "pay attention" (ESV) or "take heed" (KJV). Jesus is warning us that we should pay close attention to His teaching (doctrine). If we embrace the importance of biblical doctrine, the Lord will teach us more about Himself and His will. If we neglect His teaching, even the knowledge that we have gained will be lost. Lamentably, many Christians have not learned to appreciate the teachings of the Scriptures. We are often guilty of treating the diamonds of God's Word as though they are nothing more than pieces of coal!

3. What does Acts 2:42 teach us about the Christians in the early Church and their attitude toward doctrine?

   a. *They were* C_____ D_____ *themselves to the*

   apostles' T_____ .

NOTES: Can you imagine a church more vibrant and filled with the Holy Spirit than the one described in Acts 2? In verse 41, we read that three thousand persons were converted and baptized in one day. What was the key to such a great move of God? Although there were many factors, we know that one of the most crucial was the sincerity with which the Christians "continually devoted themselves" to the apostles' teaching. It is notable once again that the word "teaching" comes from the Greek word ***didachê***, which can also be translated, "instruction" or "doctrine" (KJV). Like the Lord Jesus Christ (Matthew 7:28-29), the apostles recognized the need to teach doctrine. The people had received pardon for their sins and the gift of the Holy Spirit (Acts 2:38), but they still needed the teaching or doctrine of the apostles to live a life pleasing to God and to be effective witnesses of the gospel.

4. According to Ephesians 4:14-15, what is another reason that Christians should be mature and instructed in Christian doctrine?

_____

_____

_____

_____

NOTES: There are more religious groups today than in any other time in the history of Christianity. We often hear about a new sect or cult proclaiming doctrines that depart from historic Christianity. Who has the truth? We can know only through an adequate comprehension of biblical doctrine. The resolution to every conflict or confusion begins with one question: "What does the Word of God have to say?"

5. What exhortation does the Apostle Paul give to his young disciple Timothy in I Timothy 4:16? How does his admonition demonstrate the importance of doctrine?

_____

_____

_____

_____

NOTES: The word "teaching" is derived from the Greek word *didaskalía*, which can also be translated, "instruction" or "doctrine" (KJV). How important is doctrine? In one way, it is accurate to say that our salvation depends upon it! Faith is not sufficient to save unless it is placed in something or someone that is worthy of it and that has the power to save us. Doctrine is important because it leads us to the true Savior, explains to us who He is, and teaches us what He requires of us.

6. According to I Timothy 6:3, what are some key characteristics that will help us identify true biblical doctrine?

    a. *It will not be a* D_____ D_____ *from that which was taught by the apostles. From the Greek word* **heterodidaskaléō** (**héteros** = different or other + **didáskō** = to teach).

b. *It will agree with S_____ words of our Lord Jesus Christ.* From the Greek word **hugiaínō**, which refers to that which is healthy, in contrast to that which is sick or sickly. True biblical doctrine will lead to spiritual health.

c. *It will be conformed or according to G_____.* From the Greek word **eusébeia**, which refers to piety, reverence, and devotion to God. True doctrine will always agree with and lead to true piety.

CHRISTIANITY IS A RELIGION OF THE HEART AND THE INTELLECT

The following declaration is commonly heard within contemporary Christianity: "Christianity is not knowledge of doctrine or a textbook of biblical facts; it is a religion of the heart—a personal relationship between God and His people." Although this frequent description of the Christian faith contains an element of truth, it also contains an element of error. While it is true that Christianity is a religion of the heart and that its highest expression is a personal relationship with God, it is equally true that Christianity is a religion of the intellect that is founded upon an accurate knowledge of biblical doctrine. In a biblical and vibrant Christianity, there is no divorce between the emotions and the intellect or between experience and the absolute truths of Scripture. They both have essential roles, and neither can be neglected without great harm to the believer and to the Church.

1. "Follow your heart!" is a common mantra heard in the world and even in the Church. How biblical is this advice? According to Jeremiah 17:9, how trustworthy are the emotions and sentiments of the heart?

_____

_____

_____

_____

2. The emotions of our heart can be completely mistaken, and they are subject to change like the wind. The Christian who directs his life according to them will be unstable and unsure in everything he does. Do you believe that the heart, unguided by biblical doctrine, is a trustworthy guide for the Christian life? How does Proverbs 14:12 warn anyone who would dare to guide his life by the emotions and sentiments of his heart?

_____

_____

_____

_____

_____

3. The heart (*i.e.* emotions and sentiments) is a very important and beautiful part of the Christian life, but it is not a sufficient guide for the Christian. We must also employ the mind (*i.e.* intellect) and grow in our knowledge of the Bible and its doctrine. According to Mark 12:30, what is one of the most critical elements of our human constitution with which we are to love and serve God?

   a. *And you shall love the Lord your God with all your heart, and with all your soul, and with*

   all your M_____, and with all your strength.

   > **NOTES:** The word "mind" comes from the Greek word *diánoia*, which may also be translated, "intellect" or "understanding." With our minds, we must grow in the knowledge of God and His will, so that we might truly love Him and serve Him as He commands. This knowledge is revealed to our minds through the Scriptures.

4. The mind is not only essential in understanding God's attributes and will, but it is also the means through which the Christian is transformed into the image of Christ. According to Romans 12:2, how can the Christian escape conformity to the world and be transformed into the image of Christ?

   _____

   _____

   _____

   _____

   > **NOTES:** Our growth in the knowledge of God's will and our increasing transformation and conformity to the image of Christ will begin with the renewal of our minds. Such a renewal is made possible through reading, studying, and meditating on the Scriptures.

5. Read Colossians 1:9-12 until you are familiar with its contents. Afterwards, answer the following questions.

   a. *According to verse 9, what does the Apostle Paul pray for the church in Colossae?*

   (1) That the believer be filled with the K_____ of God's will in all spiritual W_____ and U_____.

b. *According to verses 10-12, what would be the result of the Christian's growth in the knowledge of God's will, spiritual wisdom, and understanding?*

_____

_____

_____

_____

6. According to II Peter 1:5, what should the believer supply or add to his faith and moral excellence so that he might be mature and fruitful? How does this demonstrate the importance of the intellect and of understanding doctrine?

_____

_____

_____

_____

7. How does the Apostle Peter admonish the Church in II Peter 3:18?

a. *Grow in the G_____ and K_____ of our Lord and Savior Jesus Christ.*

NOTES: In this section of our study, we have learned a vital truth: the knowledge of biblical doctrine is an essential element in the Christian life. Knowledge of doctrine is not the goal; but it is the indispensable medium through which we achieve the goal of a life that is conformed to the image of Christ, bearing fruit to the glory of God.

Chapter 4: The Importance of Christian Doctrine

Part Two: Doctrine and the Believer

In this chapter, we will consider two more evidences of the remarkable importance of doctrine in the Christian life: (1) doctrine is the foundation and stimulant of true Christian zeal, and (2) doctrine is both practical and useful in the Christian life.

DOCTRINE IS THE FOUNDATION AND STIMULANT OF TRUE CHRISTIAN ZEAL

There are some who oppose the study of doctrine because they believe it will quench the Christian's zeal for the Lord. This belief could not be further from the truth. Though there are some theologians and scholars who have left their first love, their lack or loss of passion did not result from thoroughly studying God's Word and its doctrines. According to the Scriptures, our knowledge of the truth is the very source and catalyst of renewal and revival.

DOCTRINE IS THE SOURCE AND CATALYST OF PERSONAL REVIVAL

1. According to Luke 24:32, what did the disciples declare after the Lord Jesus Christ explained to them the things concerning Himself in all the Scriptures (v.27)?

_____

_____

_____

_____

_____

_____

NOTES: The word "burn" comes from the Greek word *kaíō*, which may also be translated, "kindle, light, or set ablaze." The Lord Jesus Christ opened up to His disciples the profound truths of Scripture concerning Himself, and their hearts were moved in an extraordinary manner. Later, these men would change the world with the truths they had heard (Acts 17:6)!

2. In Psalm 119:25, what did King David ask of God when his heart was cast down and clinging to the dust? What does this teach us about the power of God's Word and its doctrine to fill our hearts with new life and zeal?

_____

_____

_____

_____

NOTES: The idea here is twofold. David is asking that God might revive him according to the many promises that He has given in His Word and that He might revive him through or by means of His Word.

Doctrine Is the Source and Catalyst of National and Congregational Revival

1. Under the leadership of King Josiah, and later under Nehemiah, Israel experienced two of the greatest revivals in its history. According to the following texts, what was one of the primary factors that led to these awakenings? What does this teach about the role of biblical truth in revival?

   a. _II Kings 22:8-13; 23:1-14_

   _____

   _____

   _____

   _____

   b. _Nehemiah 8:1-6_

   _____

   _____

   _____

   _____

NOTES: Is it not interesting that each revival was the result of a rediscovery of God's Word? Biblical doctrine is the foundation for true revival. As we grow in our knowledge of who God is and what He has done for us, we will grow in our zeal for Him and His kingdom. The book of Psalms is a collection of worship songs, and yet it contains some of the most profound teachings regarding the person and work of God. Romans 1-11 is possibly the greatest doctrinal discourse in all of the Scriptures, and yet it culminates in one of the most beautiful and passionate expressions of praise in the entire Bible (11:33-36). The Apostle Paul was the greatest theologian in the history of the Church, and yet he was also its most zealous Christian and fruitful missionary! His doctrine was a significant factor in his zeal, love, and service for the Lord. If we desire to imitate Paul, we should give more attention to the sound doctrine that shaped his life, set his heart ablaze, and guided his actions.

2. Throughout history and until today, every genuine revival has been the result of the people of God returning to the Word of God. In the Scriptures and throughout the history of the Church, we find five prominent factors in true revival, each of which is directly related to biblical doctrine.

   a. *A VISION OF GOD AS HE IS* – Revival cannot occur without a correct view of God and His work. In general, genuine devotion begins to wane or diminish when the Church begins to depart from a biblical view of God and attempts to remake God in its own image. Today, the Church's lack of zeal and true devotion is directly related to an ignorance of the person of God. How many Christians have ever studied the doctrine of God or had the privilege of listening to a prolonged sermon series regarding His attributes and work?

   b. *A VISION OF MAN AS HE IS* – Revival is born out of need. The sinner must recognize his need of pardon before he can be saved, and the Christian must recognize his constant need of God before he can experience genuine revival. How can we recognize our true spiritual condition apart from the Scriptures and its doctrine? As sinners, we have the tendency to cover our sin, soften the commands of God, and think too highly of ourselves. For these reasons, we need the sound doctrine of God's Word to bring our sin to light and expose our need. We must learn biblical doctrine to guide our behavior and correct us when we go astray.

   c. *A RETURN TO PRAYER AND WORSHIP* – In the Scriptures and throughout Church history, a biblical devotional life is one of the most important factors in genuine revival. Today, there seems to be a renewed interest in prayer and worship, and for this we should give thanks to God. However, we must ask ourselves if we are practicing our devotions according to the Scriptures and sound doctrine. How much of all that we do is biblical? Have we investigated God's Word to discover what He desires? We would do well to remember that God once condemned two men who did not worship Him according to His Word (Leviticus 10:1-3) and that the disciples asked Jesus to teach them to pray (Luke 11:1). Genuine revival, whether personal or corporate, is directly related to prayer and worship. However, both of these devotions must be guided not by personal whims or the dictates of culture, but by the sound doctrine of God's Word.

d. *THE DIRECTION AND EMPOWERMENT OF THE HOLY SPIRIT* – The Holy Spirit is the conduit of genuine revival. Submission to His will results in life, power, and fruitfulness; but insensibility to His leadership results in spiritual barrenness. In order to experience true awakening or revival, we must recognize the Spirit's sovereignty in the Church and obey His voice. How can we recognize the work and direction of the Holy Spirit in our lives? The Scriptures teach us that there are many deceptive spirits in the world (I John 4:1) and that their activity will even increase in the latter days (I Timothy 4:1-2). How can we know that we are truly following the Holy Spirit? We can only know this by comparing every thought, teaching, and work to the sound doctrine of the Scriptures. The Holy Spirit will never contradict the Bible that He Himself inspired!

e. *OBEDIENCE* – Obedience to God's will is the crowning evidence of every genuine revival. Regardless of the attention given to worship, the height of our emotions, or the working of supposed miracles—if there is no obedience to the will of God, there is no revival. Every time we read of an awakening in the Scriptures or of a genuine revival in the history of the Church, the result is always the same—genuine submission to the Word of God and its doctrine.

DOCTRINE IS BOTH PRACTICAL AND USEFUL FOR THE CHRISTIAN LIFE

It is propagated by some Christians that doctrine is not of any real practical use in the daily Christian life. However, the following three examples demonstrate that doctrine is both practical and useful—and indeed indispensable—for the Christian life.

First, without a biblical knowledge (doctrine) of God and His works, it would be impossible to trust Him in the midst of the daily needs, problems, and trials of life. **Second**, without a biblical view (doctrine) of salvation, it would be impossible to have the peace and assurance that come from knowing that our eternal destiny is certain. **Third**, without biblical instruction (doctrine) regarding the will of God, it would be impossible to know and obey the will of God in our personal lives, our family, our church, our work, our education, or any other area.

From only three simple examples, it is evident that the study of biblical doctrine is useful, practical, and indispensable for the Christian life. The Scriptures alone are a sure foundation for our beliefs and actions.

1. What does Deuteronomy 4:5-8 teach us regarding the practical blessings that flow from a proper understanding and application of the doctrines of God's Word?

_____

_____

_____

_____

_____

2. What does Deuteronomy 32:46-47 teach us about the importance of the Scriptures' doctrine in our lives? How should we live in response to this truth?

_____

_____

_____

_____

3. According to the following texts, how can the Bible and its doctrine have a positive impact upon our daily lives as Christians?

a. *Joshua 1:8*

_____

_____

_____

_____

b. *Psalm 1:1-3*

_____

_____

_____

_____

c. *Psalm 119:105*

_____

_____

_____

_____

d. *James 1:25*

_____

_____

_____

_____

4. What did the Lord Jesus Christ teach in Matthew 7:24-28 about the importance of the Word of God and its practical application in the Christian life?

_____

_____

_____

_____

_____

_____

NOTES: The wisdom of the Scriptures should not be limited to the activities of the Church or the so-called "religious life." The Bible is a manual for the Christian's entire life. Through its doctrine, we can learn to live before God and man in a way that is pleasing to God and will bring honor to Him. The Bible teaches us to pray **and** to direct our families; it teaches us to tithe **and** to manage our personal finances; it teaches us how to conduct ourselves in the Church **and** in the world. The Scriptures speak to very practical matters in the daily life of modern man. The Bible is **the book** for every age, every circumstance, and every person. We would do well to pay close attention to God's admonition in Deuteronomy 32:47: "For it is not an idle word for you; indeed it is your life."

Chapter 5: The Importance of Christian Doctrine

Part Three: Doctrine and the Church

In this chapter, we will consider two final evidences of the great importance of doctrine in the Christian life: (1) doctrine separates light from darkness; and (2) doctrine is for every Christian, from the most mature saint to the most recent convert.

DOCTRINE SEPARATES LIGHT FROM DARKNESS

It is lamentable that at times Christians fight and divide because of doctrine. Christian unity is an essential aspect of the Christian life, and it should be protected—but not at all costs. In other words, unity must not be maintained at the cost of the doctrines that define biblical Christianity. Should we make the doctrine of the Trinity a non-essential in order to maintain unity with those who deny it? What about the blood of Christ? Salvation by faith? The authority of the Scriptures? Of course not! Although division is always painful, it is sometimes necessary. In the following texts, this truth will become clear.

1. What does Jude 3 teach us about the Christian's responsibility toward biblical doctrine and its preservation?

_____

_____

_____

_____

_____

NOTES: In this context, the word "faith" refers to the fundamental beliefs or doctrines of the Christian faith. The word "contend" comes from the Greek word **epagōnízomai**, which means, "to extend strenuous effort on behalf of something." It may also be translated, "combat" or "struggle." The Christian must not be indifferent regarding doctrine or passive when he sees it being corrupted. The phrase, "once for all handed down," denotes that Christian doctrine is fixed and should remain unmodified. We must not disregard certain truths from the Scriptures because culture says they are antiquated or archaic, nor should we add to God's Word some "new truth" recently discovered.

2. According to the following texts, when is it necessary to separate from others who also profess to be Christians?

   a. *Romans 16:17-18*

_____

_____

_____

_____

NOTES: The phrase, "the teaching which you learned," refers to the fundamental doctrines of the Christian faith that were taught by the apostles and those within their fellowship.

   b. *II John 9-11*

_____

_____

_____

_____

NOTES: This prohibition against receiving false teachers is severe but necessary. To properly understand it, we must recognize a couple of crucial truths. First, this text does not prohibit the Christian from demonstrating common courtesy to all men; rather, it prohibits us from associating and identifying with the ministry and teaching of false teachers. Secondly, the reference is made to false teachers who deny the fundamental doctrines that define the Christian faith, such as the deity of Christ (v.9). This prohibition does not refer to those who are faithful to the fundamental doctrines of the Christian faith but differ with us in the interpretation of minor doctrines or non-essentials.

   c. *I Timothy 6:3-5*

_____

_____

_____

_____

NOTES: Verse 3 provides us with an important key to identifying false doctrine. A false doctrine is any which (1) does not agree with the teachings of our Lord Jesus Christ, and (2) does not reflect or produce true godliness (*i.e.* true piety, devotion, and reverence toward God).

d. *II Thessalonians 3:6*

_____

_____

_____

_____

NOTES: Up to now, the texts that we have studied refer primarily to doctrine or teaching. This particular text also refers to ethics or behavior. It proves that we should separate not only from false teachers but also from those who claim to be Christians and yet manifest a lifestyle or behavior that is contrary to sound doctrine. At the same time, we must remember the words of the Apostle Paul in I Corinthians 5:9-11: "I wrote you in my letter not to associate with immoral people; I did not at all mean with the immoral people of this world, or with the covetous and swindlers, or with idolaters, for then you would have to go out of the world. But actually, I wrote to you not to associate with any so-called brother if he is an immoral person, or covetous, or an idolater, or a reviler, or a drunkard, or a swindler—not even to eat with such a one."

3. From what you have learned from the Scriptural texts in this chapter, explain why division is sometimes necessary.

_____

_____

_____

_____

NOTES: The purpose of doctrine is not to divide but to unite the Church. However, at times, it may be necessary to separate over fundamental doctrines of faith and practice. While we are on this side of heaven, there will always be differences between us; therefore, we must learn to walk in humility and mercy toward all. Nevertheless, there are certain fundamental doctrines that define Christianity; we must defend these, even if doing so results in division. Examples of these fundamental and non-negotiable doctrines are: *The Authority of the Bible* – The Scriptures are inspired, infallible, and absolutely authoritative in every matter of faith and practice. *The Trinity* – The one true God exists in three distinct and equal Persons: the Father, Son, and Holy Spirit. *The Universality of Sin* – All men are born with a fallen nature inherited from the first man, Adam. This fallen nature results in rebellion against God and disobedience to His law. All men are sinners and in need of reconciliation with God. *The Incarnation of the Son of God* – Two thousand years ago, the eternal Son of God was conceived in the womb of a virgin and was born the God-Man, Jesus of Nazareth. He was fully God and fully man. *The Death of Christ* – Jesus Christ, the eternal Son of God, carried our sins upon the cross of Calvary and died in our place as a substitutionary sacrifice. His death satisfied the demands of God's justice against us, appeased the wrath of God toward us, and made it possible for God to maintain His justice while pardoning the guilty. *The Resurrection of Jesus Christ* – After three days in the tomb, Jesus Christ was raised from the dead with the same physical body that had died. His resurrection was a real event in human history. *Salvation by Faith* – The redeeming work of Christ was perfect. We have neither need nor ability to add anything to it for our salvation. Salvation is by grace through faith, and it is not of our own merit—it is the gift of God (Ephesians 2:8-9). There is only one Mediator between God and men (I Timothy 2:5), and there is only one name given to men by whom they must be saved—Jesus Christ (Acts 4:12). *The Holy Spirit* – The Holy Spirit is God, the third Person of the Trinity; He dwells in the heart of everyone who is genuinely converted through faith in the Lord Jesus Christ. *The Second Coming* – Jesus Christ will come to earth again to save His Church and to judge the world. His coming will be visible, corporal, and known to all. *Heaven and Hell* – Every human being will live forever in one of two places—heaven or hell. The redeemed will spend eternity in heaven in the favorable presence of God. The unbelieving will spend eternity in hell, excluded from the favorable presence of God.

DOCTRINE IS FOR EVERY BELIEVER

One of the most frequent excuses for the Christian's neglect of doctrine is that it is simply too difficult for the "common" believer. However, this excuse is in direct contradiction to the Scriptures. All that God has revealed in His Word is for every believer. It is true that God has gifted some Christians with an unusual capacity to comprehend His revelation and that He has also granted others the privilege of studying in universities and seminaries. Nevertheless, we must always remember that our knowledge of God and His will does not depend upon our intellectual capacity or privilege as much as it depends upon our desire to know and do His will.

1. According to the Lord Jesus Christ in John 7:17, who can grow in the knowledge of God and His will? What is the requirement for growth?

_____

_____

_____

_____

_____

NOTES: It is interesting that the knowledge of Christian doctrine is more a matter of the will than of the intellect. The Christian who has made the decision to submit himself in obedience to the will of God will grow in His knowledge of the things of God. The one who searches for knowledge without commitment to obedience will learn little.

2. The Scriptures contain many promises of wisdom and knowledge for all the people of God. These apply to both the professor in the seminary and the most recent convert. What do the following texts promise to all who sincerely seek to know God and His doctrine?

   a. *Matthew 11:25*

_____

_____

_____

_____

NOTES: The "wise and the intelligent" is a reference to those who are intellectually and spiritually proud and do not recognize their need to learn from Christ. The term "infants" refers to the humble—those who recognize their needs and sincerely seek the truth from Christ. I Corinthians 3:18 contains sound advice for those who truly desire to grow in their knowledge of biblical doctrine: "Let no man deceive himself. If any man among you thinks that he is wise in this age, he must become foolish, so that he may become wise." In other words, he who believes that he is well-learned or enlightened should recognize that he knows nothing. Such humility, accompanied by the sincere study of God's Word, will lead to a genuine knowledge that transforms.

b. *I John 5:20*

_____

_____

_____

_____

NOTES: Jesus Christ is the greatest revelation of the person and will of God. To truly grow in the knowledge of God, we should look to Christ "in whom are hidden all the treasures of wisdom and knowledge" (Colossians 2:3). Through Christ's life and teaching and through the Holy Spirit, whom He gives to every believer, we can know God and sound doctrine.

c. *John 14:25-26*

_____

_____

_____

_____

NOTES: We have included this promise because it is often taken out of its original context and misapplied. In the immediate and primary context, Jesus is referring to the Holy Spirit's role in guiding the apostles into all truth, especially with regard to the writing of the New Testament (II Timothy 3:16; II Peter 1:20-21). God has not promised to inspire every believer so that his doctrine might be infallible; however, He has promised to lead and illuminate every believer by the Holy Spirit so that he might understand the inspired text written by the apostles (John 16:13; I John 2:27).

d. *I John 2:27*

_____

_____

_____

_____

_____

NOTES: The word "anointing" comes from the Greek word *chrísma* and is a reference to the Holy Spirit, who dwells in every believer (Romans 8:9). The Holy Spirit is the "Teacher of teachers" and is capable of teaching the Christian everything he needs to know about God and His will. The phrase, "you have no need for anyone to teach you," does not mean that we have no need of teachers in our churches, as Ephesians 4:11 makes it clear that God has given teachers for "the equipping of the saints." Furthermore, John himself was teaching them through his letter. The phrase simply means that the believers were not utterly dependent upon others to instruct them (Hebrews 8:11)—especially not the false teachers who had entered churches with teaching contrary to that of the apostles! Every believer can benefit from the teaching and instruction of those who have been called of God to carry out such a ministry. However, the believer is not completely dependent upon the explanations of men. Through the Holy Spirit, we can all learn from our own private study of the Scriptures.

3. According to the following Scriptures, how should we respond when we encounter a text or biblical doctrine that is difficult for us to understand?

   a. *Pray (Matthew 7:7-8; James 1:5-6)*

   _____

   _____

   _____

   _____

   b. *Seek Counsel (Acts 8:30-31; 18:23-26)*

   _____

   _____

   _____

_____

_____

NOTES: There are two extremes in studying the Scriptures. The first extreme is to study the Scriptures without consulting anyone about our interpretation or comparing our interpretation to that of other sincere believers. The second extreme is to learn from other believers, commentaries, and other sources without ever studying the Bible for ourselves. Both of these extremes are equally dangerous. The proper approach is balanced—both studying the Scriptures for ourselves and comparing our conclusions with those of contemporary believers and believers throughout Church history.

4. Having been given so many wonderful promises, what should our attitude be toward the Word of God and its doctrine? What does II Timothy 2:15 teach us?

_____

_____

_____

_____

_____

_____

PART TWO

THE HOLY SCRIPTURES

Chapter 6: An Overview of Divine Revelation

THE DEFINITION OF REVELATION

In this chapter, we will consider the **revelation of God**—the ways through which God has revealed Himself or made Himself known to mankind. We will begin by considering the definition of revelation in general and of divine revelation in particular.

>**Revelation:** The manifestation of what was before hidden or unknown. The Greek word is **apokálupsis**, which may be translated, "unveiling" or "manifestation." The verb **apokalúptō** means, "to open the curtain or unveil."

>**Divine Revelation:** The self-manifestation of God and His will to men. It is a sovereign and gracious act of God in which He opens the curtain between Himself and us so that we might know who He is, what He does, and what He demands. Throughout history, divine revelation has taken many forms (an audible voice, visions, miracles, etc.). The greatest ever revelation of God happened in the incarnation of His Son. The greatest revelation that the Christian possesses today is the Bible.

THE IMPORTANCE OF DIVINE REVELATION

Divine revelation is of crucial importance to man because man is totally incapable of knowing God through his own efforts, intelligence, or spirituality. Man cannot find God or understand His will unless God acts first to reveal Himself to man. The reason for this inability can be traced back to the fall of man through Adam. Adam was created in the image of God that he might know Him, fellowship with Him, and carry out His will upon the earth. The image of God in Adam was terribly disfigured in the fall, and he became morally corrupt. This disfigurement and moral corruption has been inherited by all of Adam's descendants. For this reason, though all men know enough about God to be without excuse, their moral corruption and hostility toward God lead them to ignore or reject all forms of revelation. For man to be saved, God must not only reveal Himself to man, but He must also work in the heart of man so that he might respond in obedience to the revelation that he has received.

1. According to Romans 3:23, what is the great spiritual malady that affects every man? What is the meaning of the phrase, "fall short of the glory of God"?

_____

_____

_____

_____

_____

NOTES: This is one of the most pivotal texts in the Bible, because it explains what man is and shows us his greatest need. Man was created in the image of God (Genesis 1:27) and for God's glory (Isaiah 43:7). However, because of sin, the image of God in man has been disfigured; man no longer possesses the will to glorify or honor God.

2. According to the following texts, what is the result of man's sin? How does man's sinful condition affect his capacity and desire to know God? Can man know God apart from a previous revelation of God and a work of grace in his heart?

   a. *Romans 1:21-22*

   _____

   _____

   _____

   _____

   b. *Ephesians 4:17-19*

   _____

   _____

   _____

   _____

THE REVELATION OF GOD

The Scriptures clearly teach that man's understanding has been corrupted by sin to the extent that he cannot know God or comprehend His will unless God first acts on his behalf. In other words, man cannot reach up to God through his own understanding; therefore, God has reached down to man through His gracious self-revelation. This revelation can be divided into two distinct categories: *general revelation* and *special revelation*. Below we will consider brief definitions and examples of both of these categories of revelation. In the next chapter, we will consider general revelation in depth; in the following chapter, we will consider special revelation in depth.

GENERAL REVELATION

This kind of revelation refers to what God has revealed about Himself and His will through nature, human intuition, the conscience, and the general course of human history. This kind of revelation is called "general" for two reasons.

1. **It is universal or accessible to all men throughout all time.** All men know intuitively that God exists (Romans 1:19), all men are born with a conscience that either approves or disapproves of their conduct (Romans 2:15), and all men can behold the evidence of God in creation (Psalm 19; Romans 1:19-20).

2. **It provides a general knowledge of God and His existence.** From general revelation, man can understand that God exists and that He is, for example, all-powerful and just.

SPECIAL REVELATION

This kind of revelation refers to the direct intervention of God into the world of men. God "breaks into" our world and reveals Himself to men through supernatural communications, direct acts of providence, the incarnation of Christ, the Scriptures, and so forth. This kind of revelation is called "special" for two reasons.

1. **It is specific or accessible to specific persons in specific times.** Consider these examples: the supernatural deliverance of Israel from the bondage of Egypt; the reception of God's Law on Mount Sinai; the incarnation of the Son of God; and the inspiration of the New Testament.

2. **It provides a specific knowledge of God and His will.** Through special revelation, the redemptive plan of God in Christ is revealed, and specific commands are made known regarding God's will.

Chapter 7: General Revelation

Now that we have taken a broad look at the revelation of God, we will spend the next two chapters looking more specifically at the two types of divine revelation: general revelation and special revelation. **General revelation** refers to what God has revealed about Himself through nature, human intuition, the conscience, and the general course of human history. It is called "general" because it is given to all men and because it provides only a limited or general revelation of God.

EXAMPLES OF GENERAL REVELATION

CREATION

God is the Creator of all things—the heavens, the earth, and all their inhabitants. Therefore, it is not strange that we find the fingerprints of the Creator throughout His creation. Through contemplating creation, man can affirm the existence and power of God.

1. What does Psalm 19:1-4 teach us about the revelation of God through creation?

_____

_____

_____

_____

_____

NOTES: This Psalm contains a beautiful poetic paradox. We read in verse 2 that day to day the creation "pours forth speech"; but in verse 3 we read that "there is no speech, nor are there words." This is not a contradiction but the setting forth of a powerful truth in an eloquent way: although no real voice or even sound is heard, creation is constantly giving testimony to the glory of God.

2. Romans 1:19-20 is the most important text in the Scriptures regarding the revelation of God through creation. What does Romans 1:19 teach us about all men?

    a. *That which is known about God is E_____ within them.* The phrase "within them" proves not only that the knowledge of the one true God is demonstrated through the works of creation, but also that God Himself has imprinted this knowledge upon the very heart of every man. The universe that God has made simply acts as a confirmation of what all men already know: there is one true God who is worthy of worship and obedience!

b. *For G_____ made it E_____ to them.* It is evident to all men that God exists because God has made it evident to all men. It is certain that all men have knowledge of God because God is the one who put it there! This knowledge is not dependent upon man; it is a work of God. It is not an elusive or hidden knowledge that can only be attained by those with superior powers of logic; it is a knowledge that is inherent in every man. For this reason, every man is without excuse!

3. God has not only made His existence evident **within** man, but He has also confirmed this knowledge in a magnificent way. According to Romans 1:20, how does God confirm the knowledge of His existence?

a. *Through what has been M_____.* The marvelous intricacies of the natural world around man bear witness to God's existence. There is no reasonable explanation for the wonderful and nearly infinite complexities of nature apart from intelligent design.

4. According to Romans 1:20, what can be known about God through His creation?

a. *His I_____ A_____.* Although the Scriptures bear witness that God is spirit (John 4:24) and that no one has seen Him in the fullness of His glory (John 1:18), the Scriptures also testify that His attributes or characteristics can be known through what He has made.

b. *His E_____ power and D_____ nature.* Here the "attributes" mentioned above are further defined. It is evident that our universe is not eternal but had a beginning. Furthermore, it is evident that our universe did not possess the power or wisdom to bring itself out of nothing. Therefore, there must be a Creator who precedes creation and is not subject to its limitations—a God who is both eternal and all-powerful; an uncaused Cause; an uncreated Creator; a Being who simply "is," without beginning or end. The Bible begins its account of creation with the affirmation, "In the beginning, God..." (Genesis 1:1). We read in the book of Psalms, "Before the mountains were born or You gave birth to the earth and the world, even from everlasting to everlasting, You are God" (90:2).

5. God has revealed Himself to man through creation. This revelation should lead men to recognize the power of God and to worship Him as Creator. However, according to Romans 1:21-23, how has man responded to God's revelation through creation?

_____

_____

_____

_____

NOTES: In this text, we read of the rebellious and destructive response of all men since Adam to the general revelation of God through creation. God has not hidden Himself from man, but man has hidden himself from God. He has purposely ignored or even denied God's revelation so that he might continue in his sinful rebellion.

MAN'S INTUITION

The word "intuition" comes from the Latin word *intueri* [*in* = upon + *tueri* = to look]. It refers to the ability to know or understand something without the conscious use of reason. It is an innate knowledge that is an endowment from God and is possessed without prior personal investigation or learning. From the Scriptures and from experience, we know that man possesses an intuitive or innate knowledge of God. Every nation, people, and tribe has some concept of deity; and, in spite of their obvious distortions of God, this demonstrates that the knowledge of the divine is firmly rooted in the heart of every human. Even the atheist, who professes to deny God's existence, must admit that he arrived at such a conclusion only after having first believed in God. There is something in man that recognizes the divine and the eternal and is drawn toward them. The theologian Augustine of Hippo (A.D. 354-430) explained it in this way: "You have made us for yourself, O Lord, and our heart is restless until it rests in you."[1]

1. What does Genesis 1:27 affirm about the creation of man?

   a. *God created man in His own I_____, in the I_____ of God He created him.*

   NOTES: The Scriptures declare that God created Adam and Eve in His own image, and this separates mankind from all other creatures. Since man was created in the very image of God, should we not expect him to possess an innate or intuitive knowledge of the One who made him? James teaches us that, in spite of the fall, the image of God still remains in every man (James 3:9).

2. In Romans 1:19, what do the Scriptures teach about human intuition or man's innate knowledge of God?

   a. *That which is known about God is evident W_____ them; for G_____ made it evident to them.*

   NOTES: There are two possibilities with regard to the meaning of this text. First, it could possibly mean that God has made His existence known to all men through the creation that He has made. Second, it could possibly mean that God has placed an innate or intuitive knowledge of Himself in every man, which the observable creation simply confirms. The latter interpretation seems preferable. The knowledge of God is woven into the very fabric of man's being.

---

[1] *Confessions* 1, 1: PL 32, 661

3. In Ecclesiastes 3:11 is found one of the most majestic declarations in the Scriptures with regard to man as the special creation of God. How does this text testify to man's knowledge of God?

_____

_____

_____

_____

_____

_____

NOTES: The phrase, "He has also set eternity in their heart," is one of the most beautiful descriptions of man as the special creation of God. The idea is that God has put the knowledge of eternity in the heart of man, which yields an impulse that moves man beyond the temporal and toward the eternal. For this reason, even though man may "gain the whole world" (Matthew 16:26), it will not satisfy the longing in his heart for that which is beyond the temporal and the worldly. To reiterate the wisdom of Augustine, "He has made us for Himself, and our heart is restless until it rests in Him."

4. Man was created with an innate knowledge of God, to which the rest of creation bears witness. However, according to Romans 1:18, how has man responded to this knowledge?

_____

_____

_____

_____

NOTES: The word "suppress" comes from the Greek word **katéchō**, which means, "to hold down, hold back, or restrain." Men have been endowed with an innate or intuitive knowledge of God that is verified through the glories and complexities of creation. However, instead of seeking God, fallen man has suppressed this knowledge in an attempt to shut God out of his mind so that he might freely indulge in sin.

MAN'S CONSCIENCE

The Scriptures affirm that all men possess a conscience—an innate knowledge of good and evil and the compulsion to do good. The conscience involves more than personal desires or tastes; it is an expression of the will of God, a moral law that God has put in the heart of every man. In spite of man's fallenness and the almost infinitely variant cultures of the world, there is still a general agreement regarding good and evil in every civilization. If the conscience is not rejected or misinterpreted, it can be a limited guide to direct men to God and His will.

1. According to Romans 2:14-15, what has God done to reveal His existence to all men?

   a. *God has written His L_____ on the H_____ of all men (Romans 2:15).* God created man in His own image (Genesis 1:26-27). Although this image has been seriously corrupted by sin, it has not been totally lost (Genesis 9:6; I Corinthians 11:7; James 3:9). One aspect of this image is that all humans possess an innate sense of right and wrong—God has written (Greek: **graptós**, which means, "imprinted or engraved") His law on the heart of every man. For this reason, all cultures hold to similar moral standards that reflect God's law (*e.g.* telling the truth; honoring one's parents; prohibiting murder, adultery, theft, and the like). This revelation is evidence not only of God's existence but also of His righteousness. For this reason, all men will be held accountable on the Day of Judgment.

   b. *God has given a C_____ to every man (Romans 2:15).* The conscience (Greek: **suneídēsis**) refers to still another aspect of the image of God within man; it enables him to measure his conformity to the law that God has written on his heart. This conscience defends or approves man when he obeys God's law and accuses or condemns him in every act of disobedience. Thus, the conscience serves to demonstrate man's guilt and his need of reconciliation with a righteous God.

2. God has revealed Himself to men through creation and the conscience. These should lead men to recognize Him as their Creator and to seek Him diligently. According to Romans 3:9-12, how has man responded to the revelation of God through creation?

_____

_____

_____

_____

_____

_____

3. According to the following texts of Scripture, what can happen to a person who continues to ignore or reject the conscience?

a. *Romans 1:28-32*

_____

_____

_____

_____

b. *Ephesians 4:18-19*

_____

_____

_____

_____

c. *I Timothy 4:2*

_____

_____

_____

_____

NOTES: The phrase, "seared with a branding iron," comes from the Greek verb *kautēriázō*, which means, "to burn to the point of searing with a brand or a hot iron." When human flesh is cauterized or seared, it loses all feeling or sensitivity. In a similar but more horrifying fashion, a person's conscience can become so cauterized that it loses all sensitivity to evil and is given over to it without shame.

d. *Titus 1:15*

_____

_____

_____

_____

> **NOTES:** The word "defiled" comes from the Greek word **miaíno**, which may also be translated, "polluted, stained, or depraved." The conscience is a gift from God that requires proper stewardship. If a man continues to deny the voice of his conscience and gives himself to wanton sin, the conscience can become polluted, defiled, and calloused. There is no need to prove the reality of this truth. The history books of every culture are filled with countless examples of the atrocities of men and societies whose consciences had become defiled or seared.

HUMAN HISTORY

God has revealed Himself through the annals of human history with such clarity that we can properly say that the history of man is the history of God in the world of men. Since the very dawn of time, God has been working in the world and advancing toward His goal of redemption. We do not have to contemplate human history for long before we detect His sovereign hand fulfilling His will and converting every opposing power and work into nothing. Two of the greatest examples of the revelation of God through history are the preservation of the nation of Israel and the Church. For thousands of years, Israel and the Church have been persecuted, at times almost to the point of extinction. But God always intervenes for their salvation, and both continue even today.

THE LIMITATIONS OF GENERAL REVELATION

By means of general revelation (through creation, intuition, conscience, and human history), God has revealed Himself to all men. However, general revelation in itself is insufficient for two primary reasons. First, it is limited in the knowledge that it provides. It proves that there is a God who created the universe, that He is just, and that man has violated His law; however, it does not reveal God's redemptive plan. Second, it is limited because of what man is. Fallen man is a morally corrupt creature who is hostile toward God's person and law. He desires autonomy in order to give reign to his moral corruption. Therefore, he denies the innate knowledge of God that has been bestowed upon him, he embraces the irrationality of evolution in order to cast God from His creation, he rejects the dictates of his conscience, and he ignores the repetitive lessons of human history. In order to save man, God must intervene directly in the world of man through what is known as **special revelation**.

Chapter 8: Special Revelation

General revelation refers to the revelation of God that is found in nature, man, and history. Special revelation refers to the direct intervention of God into the world of men. It is called "special" because it provides a specific and saving knowledge of God and because it has been accessible to specific peoples in specific times and places. In our study, we will consider three categories of specific revelation: supernatural manifestations, the incarnation of God's Son, and the writing of the Scriptures.

SUPERNATURAL MANIFESTATIONS

Throughout history, God has spoken to men through various supernatural means. The following are several of the most prominent.

1. THEOPHANY (Greek: **theós** = God + **phaínō** = to appear) – At times in biblical history, God has revealed Himself to men in a visible form: Abraham's visitor (Genesis 18:1-22), the man who wrestled with Jacob (Genesis 32:22-32), and the soldier who appeared to Joshua (Joshua 5:13-15) are all examples of this. God has also appeared as the Angel of the Lord to Hagar (Genesis 16:7-14), to Moses in a burning bush (Exodus 3:16), and to Samson's parents (Judges 13:17-22). Since the Scriptures declare that "no one has seen God [the Father] at any time" (John 1:18), many scholars believe that these theophanies were appearances of the second Person of the Trinity, the Son of God. It is important to recognize the difference between the theophanies of God in the Old Testament and the incarnation of God in the New Testament. In the theophanies, God manifested Himself in the **appearance of a man**. In the incarnation, God actually **became a man**, being conceived by the Holy Spirit and born of the Virgin Mary (Matthew 1:18, 20; Luke 1:35).

2. AUDIBLE VOICE – At times in the Scriptures, we find God speaking to His servants by means of an audible voice. In the Old Testament, God spoke "face to face" with Moses (Exodus 33:11; Numbers 12:5-8), He called Samuel with what seemed to be a human voice (I Samuel 3), and He spoke to Elijah with a voice that was like the sound of a gentle breeze (I Kings 19:11-13). In the New Testament, God spoke with an audible voice while bearing witness to Jesus before John the Baptist (Matthew 3:16-17), the disciples (Matthew 17:5), and a crowd (John 12:28-30).

3. VISIONS AND DREAMS – In the Scriptures, God employs dreams and visions to communicate His Word or will to His servants. Dreams and visions refer to the communication of the divine will through a series of images or thoughts. Such communications can occur when the recipient is sleeping, awake, or in a trance-like state. It is important to note that the Scriptures also warn that not all dreams and visions are from God (Deuteronomy 13:1-5). The Apostle Paul warned the church in Colossae against a preoccupation with visions (Colossians 2:18).

4. ANGELS – The word "angel" is translated from the Hebrew word **malak** and the Greek word **ággelos**. In both instances it literally means, "messenger"; therefore, it is not strange that God would employ them to communicate His will to His servants. As with the other means

of supernatural communication, the appearance of angels is a rare event that occurs only at a time of great need or during extreme circumstances. Also, it is important to note that the Scriptures warn that not all angelic communications are from God. Satan may disguise himself as an angel of light in order to deceive (II Corinthians 11:14). The Apostle Paul warned the church in Colossae against a preoccupation with angels (Colossians 2:18).

5. MIRACLES – A miracle is an extraordinary work of God that transcends nature. The biblical concept of miracles can encompass various types and kinds of events, such as destroying a city (Genesis 19:24-25), dividing a sea (Exodus 14:21-22), causing a piece of iron to float (II Kings 6:6), restoring a blind man's sight (John 9:1-12), or resurrecting a dead man (John 11:38-44). With regard to divine revelation, the purpose of a miracle is to reveal God and His will to man (Exodus 10:1-2) or to verify that a messenger or message is from God (Exodus 4:1-9; John 7:31; 10:38). As in the other cases of supernatural communications, the Bible warns that not all miracles are from God. Satan and his false prophets can also use miracles to deceive (Exodus 7:8-12; Matthew 7:21-23; Revelation 19:20).

THE INCARNATION OF THE SON OF GOD

The greatest revelation of God and His will in the history of mankind is the incarnation of His Son Jesus Christ. The word "incarnation" (Latin: **in** = into + **carn** = flesh) refers to the act of becoming flesh or assuming a body of flesh. With reference to Christian doctrine, the word "incarnation" denotes that the eternal Son of God left His glory in heaven, was conceived by the Holy Spirit, was born of a virgin, and lived upon this earth as Jesus of Nazareth—the Son of God and the Son of Man. Being fully God, He was the perfect representation of all that God is. Being fully man, He came to mankind in a manner that we could understand.

1. Hebrews 1:1-3 is one of the most important Scriptures regarding the person and work of Jesus Christ. Read the text until you are familiar with its contents, and then answer the following questions.

   a. *According to verse 1, how did God speak to His people long ago?*

   _____

   _____

   _____

   b. *According to verse 2, how has God spoken to His people in these last days?*

   _____

   _____

   _____

c. *According to verse 3, why is Jesus the most perfect or complete revelation of God and His will?*

_____

_____

_____

NOTES: The phrases, "the radiance of His glory" and "the exact representation of His nature," can also be translated, "the perfect reflection of His glory" and "the exact expression of His nature" respectively. This is an undeniable statement of Christ's deity! Since He is God, He is the most perfect or complete revelation of God!

2. In verses 1 and 14 of John 1, we find some of the most important declarations in the Bible with regard to the Son of God and the incarnation. Read the two verses carefully, and then answer the following questions.

a. *What is the name or title that is given to the Son of God in verse 1?*

(1) The W_____. From the Greek noun **lógos**, which can be translated, "word" or "discourse." Jesus is the "Word" of God and the perfect communication, revelation, or discourse of His person and will.

b. *What other great truths does verse 1 communicate to us about the Son of God?*

(1) He existed from the B_____. He is the eternal God. He was there before the world began, and He was there when the world began. He has no beginning or end.

(2) He was always with G_____. The Son is equal with the Father and existed throughout eternity in perfect fellowship with Him, but He is also a distinct Person from the Father.

(3) He was G_____. This is one of the clearest and most powerful declarations of the deity of the Son. He possessed the same essence as God. He was God in the fullest sense of the term.

c. *According to verse 1, the Son of God is the second Person of the Trinity, equal to and yet a distinct Person from the Father and the Spirit. According to John 1:14, how did the Son reveal God to man?*

(1) The Word became F_____ and D_____ among us. Jesus is the perfect revelation of God for two reasons. **First**, He is God—the perfect reflection of His glory and the exact representation of His nature. **Secondly**, He became a man—without setting aside His deity, the Son robed Himself in human flesh as a real man. The

word "dwelt" comes from the Greek word **eskênōsen**, which means, "to pitch a tent or dwell in a tent." In the Old Testament, God was present among His people in a tent or tabernacle (Exodus 33:9-10). In the incarnation, God "dwelt" or "tabernacled" among men in the body of a real man.

3. According to I John 1:1, how personal and accessible was the revelation of God through the person of Jesus Christ?

    a. *Men H_____ Him with their ears.*

    b. *Men S_____ Him with their eyes.*

    c. *Men L_____ at Him.* This statement is not redundant. The phrase "looked at" comes from the Greek word **theáomai**, which can also be translated, "to behold," "to look over," or "to watch." It denotes careful observation or contemplation. Men did not just catch a glimpse of the incarnate Son; they carefully watched and examined His life.

    d. *Men T_____ Him with their hands.* This statement is key with reference to Christ's incarnation and His resurrection. He came in a real human body, and He was raised with the same real body (John 20:25-28).

4. To conclude, what do the following biblical texts teach us about the revelation of God through His Son? How do these texts prove that He was and is the greatest of all divine revelations?

    a. *John 1:18*

    _____

    _____

    _____

    _____

    _____

    NOTES: The word "explained" comes from the Greek word **exēgéomai**, which means, "to expound, detail, set forth, make known, or reveal."

    b. *John 14:8-9*

    _____

    _____

_____

_____

_____

> **NOTES:** The Lord Jesus Christ is the greatest revelation of God and the indisputable evidence of His existence and involvement in the world. All that can be known about God is manifested in Jesus of Nazareth. No other teacher or prophet can add anything to the revelation of God that was given in Jesus. He is God revealed to us in human form (Colossians 2:9). He is the very Word of God made flesh (John 1:1, 14). Therefore, we would do well to obey God's admonition to us in Matthew 17:5: "This is my beloved Son, with whom I am well-pleased; listen to Him."

THE BIBLE

We have learned in this lesson that throughout history, God has revealed Himself and His will through various supernatural communications such as theophanies, visions, dreams, an audible voice, angels, and miracles. We have also learned that, two thousand years ago, God gave man the greatest revelation of Himself and His will through the person of Jesus Christ. Nevertheless, we are left with a critical question:

How does God speak with us today in the twenty-first century?

How can we know that what we have seen, heard, or felt is true? Upon what authority can we base our beliefs and actions? The answer is found in II Timothy 3:16-17:

> "All Scripture is inspired by God and profitable for teaching, for re-proof, for correction, for training in righteousness; so that the man of God may be adequate, equipped for every good work."

The Bible is the highest authority in the Christian life and the standard of validity for all other revelations, experiences, teachings, and ideas. Any revelation, experience, teaching, idea, attitude, or action that contradicts or is not conformed to the teaching of Scripture must be rejected. The Bible is the most important and useful revelation of God for the Christian in the twenty-first century. For this reason, we must follow and obey the admonition of the Apostle Paul in II Timothy 2:15:

> "Be diligent to present yourself approved to God as a workman who does not need to be ashamed, accurately handling the word of truth."

Chapter 9: The Trustworthiness of the Bible

In this chapter, we will consider the trustworthiness of the Bible as the infallible written revelation of God to man.

WHAT IS THE BIBLE?

The word "bible" comes from the Greek word **biblía**, which literally means, "books." The name refers to the collection of the sixty-six books of the Old and New Testaments that the Christian Church recognizes as the inspired record of the self-revelation of God and His will to man.

THE INSPIRATION OF THE BIBLE

Christians believe that the Bible is God's revelation to man and that He is its ultimate source. However, this leads to several key questions. If the Bible is from God, how did it appear in written form? If the truths of Scripture were recorded by human authors, how do we know that they did not make a mistake? To answer these questions, we point to God's wisdom, power, and providence in guiding men both to record and to preserve His revelation. Christians believe that God **inspired** the Bible. Divine inspiration refers to the supernatural influence of the Holy Spirit over the writers of the Scriptures that resulted in a totally trustworthy record of the revelation of God.

1. One of the most crucial texts regarding the trustworthiness and divine origin of the Scriptures is II Timothy 3:16. What does this text teach us?

   a. *A_____ Scripture is I_____ by God.* The word "inspired" comes from the Greek word **theópneustos**, which literally means, "God-breathed." The words of Scripture were breathed out by God. It is important to note that the doctrine of inspiration refers to **all** Scripture. Every word in the original manuscripts of the Bible was inspired and carries all the authority of the Word of God.

2. What does II Peter 1:21 teach us regarding the inspiration of the Bible and the role of men in its formation?

   _____

   _____

   _____

   _____

NOTES: The word "moved" is translated from the Greek word *phérō*, which means, "to carry" or "to bear." The Bible was inspired by God and communicated in written form through men who were "carried" or "guided" by the Holy Spirit. Based on these two truths, we can make two important observations: (1) men put the Bible in written form, so the personality and style of each author is therefore evident; and (2) the Holy Spirit guided the writers, so the Bible is therefore the inspired and inerrant revelation of God to man.

3. To bring this part of our study to a close, we will consider one last question. According to Matthew 4:4, what was the opinion of Jesus Christ with regard to the inspiration of the Scriptures?

_____

_____

_____

_____

NOTES: From the above texts, we have learned that the Bible was inspired by God and communicated to us in its written form through men who were guided by the Holy Spirit.

THE TRUSTWORTHINESS OF THE BIBLE

The fact that the Bible is the inspired and infallible Word of God has serious significance for the Christian. It means that the Bible is absolutely trustworthy, that its promises are always faithful, and that its commandments and principles are the very wisdom of God. The wise and obedient believer can build his or her life upon its every word.

1. What do the following texts teach us about the trustworthiness of God and His Word?

    a. *Numbers 23:19*

_____

_____

_____

_____

b. *Joshua 23:14*

_____

_____

_____

_____

c. *Psalm 119:137-138*

_____

_____

_____

_____

_____

NOTES: The character or nature of God's person determines the character and nature of all His works. Since God is righteous and faithful, we can expect the same from the Word that He has given us.

2. The trustworthiness of God's Word is directly related to its eternality (it endures forever) and immutability (it does not change). If the Word of God were not eternal or if its promises and commands were subject to change, it would not be trustworthy. What do the following texts teach about the eternality, immovability, and trustworthiness of God's Word?

a. *Psalm 119:89-90*

_____

_____

_____

_____

NOTES: The phrase "is settled" comes from the Hebrew verb *natsab*, which may also be translated, "firmly fixed" (ESV) or "stand secure" (NET). The phrase, "You have founded them forever," may also be translated, "You have ordained your rules to last" (NET). Notice in verse 90 that the faithfulness of God ensures the faithfulness of His works and word.

b. *Psalm 119:152*

_____

_____

_____

_____

NOTES: The word "founded" comes from the Hebrew word *yasad*, which may also be translated, "established" or "fixed." The word is used with reference to laying a foundation upon which a building is established.

c. *Isaiah 40:6-8*

_____

_____

_____

_____

d. *Luke 21:33*

_____

_____

_____

_____

3. Another truth directly related to the trustworthiness of Scripture is its infallibility or freedom from error. What do the following texts teach us about this truth?

   a. *Psalm 12:6*

   _____

   _____

   _____

   _____

   NOTES: The word "pure" comes from the Hebrew word **tahor**, which may also be translated, "clean." In the Scriptures, the number seven is a sign of completeness or perfection. Silver refined seven times is the purest of silver.

   b. *Psalm 119:140*

   _____

   _____

   _____

   _____

   NOTES: The word "pure" comes from the Hebrew verb **tsaraph**, which means, "to smelt, refine, or test." God's Word is "very pure," like silver or gold refined to its most perfect or flawless state.

   c. *Proverbs 30:5-6*

   _____

   _____

   _____

   _____

NOTES: The word "every" is absolutely vital. The Scriptures do not *contain* the Word of God; the Scriptures **are** the Word of God. The Bible is inspired not in part but in whole. The word "tested" comes from the Hebrew word **tzaraph**, which means, "to refine." It is the same word used in Psalm 12:6: "As silver tried [**tzaraph**] in a furnace on the earth, refined seven times."

4. In Psalm 19:7-9 are six different characteristics of the Scriptures that demonstrate their trustworthiness. Identify them in the following exercise.

a. *The Law of God is P_____* (v.7). From the Hebrew word **tamin**, which also denotes completeness, wholeness, and sufficiency. Although nature does reveal the glory of God (vv.1-6), the Scriptures are a more complete revelation of God.

b. *The Testimony of the Lord is S_____* (v.7). From the Hebrew word **aman**, which means, "to trust." The idea is that the Lord's testimonies are completely trustworthy and reliable.

c. *The Precepts of the Lord are R_____* (v.8). From the Hebrew word **yashar**, which may be translated, "smooth," "straight," or "upright." The Lord's precepts lead men in straight paths of righteousness. "In all your ways acknowledge Him, and He will make your paths straight [**yashar**]" (Proverbs 3:6).

d. *The Commandment of the Lord is P_____* (v.8). From the Hebrew word **bar**, which denotes purity and innocence. The commandments of God are pure because they come from a God who is altogether holy and righteous.

e. *The Fear of the Lord is C_____, enduring forever* (v.9). Here the Word of God is referenced as the fear of the Lord, probably because it teaches us to fear or revere God and because obedience to the Word is the primary means of showing reverence toward Him. The word "clean" comes from the Hebrew word **tahor**, which denotes cleanliness and purity. "The words of the Lord are pure [**tahor**] words; as silver tried in a furnace on the earth, refined seven times" (Psalm 12:6).

f. *The Judgments of the Lord are T_____ and R_____* (v.9). "The judgments of the Lord" refers to His commands. The phrase can also be translated as "the rules of the Lord" (ESV) or "the judgments given by the Lord" (NET). The word "true" is translated from the Hebrew word **'emet**, which denotes firmness, faithfulness, and truth. The word "righteous" is translated from the Hebrew word **tzadeq**, which denotes that which is just and right. The judgments of the Lord are righteous because they come from the mouth of a righteous God and lead to righteousness for all those who adhere to them.

SUMMARY

The Bible is the infallible Word of God and the absolute authority for the Christian who longs to know God and to do His will. No other book, teaching, philosophy, or tradition should be elevated over the Bible as its superior or even brought beside the Bible as its equal. The Bible is totally unique—the perfect revelation of God to man.

Chapter 10: A Brief History of the Bible

In this chapter, we will consider a brief history of the sacred Scriptures—a compilation of sixty-six books written over a period of fifteen hundred years (from the fourteenth century B.C. to the first century) by over forty authors from every walk of life. The writing and formation of the Bible is one of the most amazing demonstrations of God's providence or sovereignty in history. It is His work from beginning to end, from the inspiration of the writers to the preservation of their writings until today and forever. As Jesus declared, "Heaven and earth will pass away, but My words will not pass away" (Mark 13:31).

THE ORIGINAL MANUSCRIPTS

In the first step of the Bible's formation, God directed men to write His words in what are today called the original manuscripts. In the beginning, the Scriptures were not written in English upon fine paper with gilded edges and covered in luxurious leather. The original manuscripts were often written using rustic materials and in languages that are unknown to the great majority of us today.

THE ORIGINAL MATERIALS

The authors of the Bible used various types of material to preserve the Word of God, which they received under the direction of the Holy Spirit.

STONE

The first two tablets of the Ten Commandments were written upon stone by the finger of God (Exodus 24:12; 31:18; 32:15-16; 34:1, 28; Deuteronomy 4:13; 5:22). At that time, words were often engraved upon stone with a chisel.

WOOD

Words were engraved with a chisel upon wooden tablets. Often, the words were engraved upon wax that covered the tablet. The wax could then be cleaned, and a new message could be written on the same tablet (Isaiah 8:1; 30:8; Habakkuk 2:2; Luke 1:63).

PAPYRUS

Papyrus was made of split cane that was pressed together to form a material similar to rough paper. It was then bound together into a roll of about twenty pages. Words were written upon the papyrus with a thin reed and ink. References to papyrus are found in II John 12, II Timothy 4:13, and Revelation 5:1.

PARCHMENT

Parchment was made of cured goatskin or sheepskin. The Scriptures were commonly recorded on parchment, which began to replace papyrus around 200 B.C. A reference to parchment is found in II Timothy 4:13. To make a New Testament of parchment required fifty to sixty sheep and was very costly.

THE ORIGINAL LANGUAGES

Our English Bibles are translations from the original manuscripts, which were written in the common languages of their authors. The Old Testament was written primarily in Hebrew, while the New Testament was written in Greek.

HEBREW

The Old Testament was written in Hebrew, with the exception of a few Aramaic texts.[2] Hebrew is a Semitic language with twenty-two consonants. Originally, it was written without vowels until a group of Jewish scholars called **Masoretes** (or traditionalists) added vowels to aid in the pronunciation of the text (A.D. 600-950). Hebrew grammar is simple, and the vocabulary is not extensive; however, it is a very descriptive and picturesque language. The following example is taken from Psalm 23:1 as it appears in the Hebrew Bible. It is read from right to left:

א רוֹמְזִמ דְוָדְל: הָוֹהְי יֵעֹר, אֹל רָסְחֶא.

GREEK

The entire New Testament was written in the Greek language. In the period in which the New Testament was written, there were two dialects of Greek: (1) **Attic Greek** – the classic or prestige dialect that was spoken in the Attic Peninsula, where Athens was located; and (2) **Koine Greek** – from the Greek word meaning "common," **Koine** was the dialect used for the New Testament writings and is also known as the Alexandrian dialect, common Attic, or Hellenistic Greek. It was the language of the common man in the Greco-Roman world from 300 B.C. to A.D. 300. The language is characterized by simplicity of form and syntax, precision, and clarity. The following example is taken from John 3:16 as it appears in the Greek New Testament. It is read from left to right:

Οὕτως γὰρ ἠγάπησεν ὁ θεὸς τὸν κόσμον, ὥστε τὸν υἱὸν τὸν μονογενῆ ἔδωκεν, ἵνα πᾶς ὁ πιστεύων εἰς αὐτὸν μὴ ἀπόληται ἀλλ᾽ ἔχῃ ζωὴν αἰώνιον.

THE ORIGINAL FORM

Originally, the books of the Bible did not have chapters or verses. In 1228, Steven Lanton, the Archbishop of Canterbury, divided the Bible into chapters. The first Bible with the modern divisions of chapters and verses was published as an edition of the Latin Vulgate by Robert Estienne in Paris in 1551. The purpose of dividing the books of the Bible into chapters and verses was to facilitate their reading.

ANCIENT COPIES

The original manuscripts of the Bible, written by the hand of their authors or secretaries, no longer exist. Therefore, it is necessary to rely upon the ancient copies that we do possess. This gives rise to the following question: How do we know that the ancient copies in our possession are faithful reproductions of the originals? The answer is twofold. **First**, the same God that in-

---

[2] Ezra 4:8-6:18; 7:12-26; Jeremiah 10:11; Daniel 2:4-7:28

spired the Scriptures is sovereign and powerful to preserve them in the copies. **Second**, the comparison of more than two thousand ancient complete and partial copies of the Old Testament, along with approximately five thousand copies of the New Testament and ten thousand copies of early versions, provides indisputable evidence that the Bible we have today is a faithful reproduction of the original manuscripts. No document of antiquity is as highly attested as the Bible.

ANCIENT COPIES OF THE OLD TESTAMENT

The reverence of the ancient Jews for the Word of God together with the work of the scribes who dedicated themselves to the transmission of the Old Testament resulted in its faithful reproduction in the more than two thousand complete and partial ancient copies we possess today. Even though there are minimal variations in the different copies, the original text can be recomposed through the following means: (1) by careful comparison of the copies, especially those that are most ancient; and (2) by studying the Old Testament citations that are found in the New Testament and in literature outside of the Scriptures. The following are some of the most significant copies of the Old Testament.

THE DEAD SEA SCROLLS

In 1947, hundreds of Hebrew manuscripts were found in the Qumran caves near the Dead Sea. A Jewish sect known as the Essenes probably hid them in the caves during the second or first century B.C. The manuscripts contain fragments of the entire Old Testament with the exception of Esther. The manuscripts have been dated sometime during the second and first centuries B.C. They are one thousand years older than any manuscript previously discovered and yet are nearly identical to later copies. Thus, they demonstrate the faithful replication of the original manuscripts.

THE SEPTUAGINT (LXX)

The Septuagint is the Greek version of the Hebrew Old Testament. According to tradition, it was translated between 280-150 B.C. in Alexandria, Egypt, by seventy Jewish scholars—hence the name "Septuagint," derived from the Latin word for seventy (**septuaginta**). The purpose of the translation was to provide the Scriptures to Jews who did not speak Hebrew. The Septuagint was commonly used in the time of Jesus and was adopted by the early Church. Most of the Old Testament quotes in the New Testament are taken from the Septuagint.

THE MASORETIC TEXT

The Masoretic Text was copied by a group of Jewish scholars known as the **Masoretes** or **Traditionalists** (Hebrew: **masoreth** = tradition). Prior to the sixth century, the Hebrew manuscripts were consonantal (containing only consonants and no vowels). Between the sixth and tenth centuries, the Masoretes invented a system of vowels and accents to preserve the correct pronunciation of the text. These vowels and accents were added to the Hebrew manuscripts, along with textual variations that were written in the margins.

ANCIENT COPIES OF THE NEW TESTAMENT

The ancient copies of the New Testament can be divided according to two distinct categories: (1) according to their date and the material upon which the copies were written; and (2) according to their similarities or common characteristics.

DATE AND MATERIAL

The Greek copies of the original New Testament manuscripts that we possess today were made in different centuries and utilized different materials. There are three primary groups or classifications.

Papyri: Greek manuscripts from the second and third centuries that were written on papyrus.

Uncials: Greek manuscripts copied between the fourth and ninth centuries that were written with all uppercase (or capital) letters, no spaces between words, and no punctuation. The following is an example of uncial writing from John 1:1 ("In the beginning was the Word, and the Word..."):

$$ΕΝΑΡΧΗΗΝΟΛΟΓΟΣΚΑΙΟΛΟΓΟΣ$$

Minuscules: Greek manuscripts copied between the ninth and fifteenth centuries that were written with uppercase and lowercase letters. The following is an example of minuscule writing from John 1:1 ("In the beginning was the word, and the word..."):

$$Ἐν ἀρχῇ ἦν ὁ Λόγος , καὶ ὁ Λόγος$$

SIMILARITIES OR COMMON CHARACTERISTICS

In the early Church, after an Epistle or Gospel was sent to a congregation or an individual, copies were made and sent to other nearby congregations. Through this process, it was inevitable that eventually these handwritten copies contained small variations or differences from one another. The majority of these differences were the result of a scribal error or an attempt by the scribe to clarify the meaning of a difficult text. When an established church that possessed a copy of the Scriptures started a new congregation, they would make another copy for the new church to use. Later, more copies would be made from the same copy and would be sent to other new congregations nearby. With time, the manuscripts used by the churches in the same area contained the same characteristics and variations. For this reason, scholars can now group the various ancient manuscripts into different families by comparing them to the biblical citations found in the writings of the pastors and theologians who lived in the different ecclesiastical (church) centers. Four of the most significant families or groups are listed below.

The Byzantine Text (also called Majority Text, Antiochene Text, or Syrian Text): This text is characterized by its clarity and detail. From the seventh century to the invention of the printing press (A.D. 1450-1456), the Byzantine text was the most accepted and most highly circulated text. It is the basis of the **Textus Receptus** prepared by Erasmus in 1516 and the King James Version.

The Alexandrian Text: This text is characterized by its brevity and conciseness. It was heavily used in the translation of the New American Standard Bible, the English Standard Version, and the New King James Bible.

The Western Text: This text was circulated in Italy, Gaul, Northern Africa, and Egypt. The renowned Church fathers Irenaeus, Tertullian, and Cyprian used this text. The

Western text is characterized by its length and use of parentheses. Words, phrases, and sentences are changed, removed, and added in order to clarify, harmonize, and enrich the meaning.

The Caesarean Text (also called the Egyptian Text): This text probably originated in Egypt. It is believed that Origen brought a copy to Caesarea, where Eusebius and others used it. From Caesarea, it was carried to Jerusalem, where Cyril used it. The Caesarean text could be categorized as a middle ground between the Alexandrian and Western texts.

THE BEST TEXT

Having read the above section, we might ask, "How can we determine which text is closest to the original document?" The scholars who give themselves to this exacting and meticulous labor base their decisions upon the following considerations.

1. THE DATE OF THE TEXT – All other factors being equal, the oldest text is usually preferred. An early date reduces the potential of variants.

2. EASE OF READING – The text that is most difficult to read is usually preferred over the text that is more reader-friendly. Ancient scribes had a tendency to adjust the texts they were copying in order to make them easier to read and understand.

3. THE LENGTH OF THE TEXT – The text that is shortest or more concise is usually preferred. Ancient scribes had a tendency to add words or phrases in order to clarify a text or make it more readable.

4. APPARENT CONTRADICTIONS – The text that contains more paradoxes—apparent contradictions—is usually preferred. Some ancient scribes had a tendency to alter texts that **appeared** contradictory or **seemed** difficult to harmonize. This was due to the scribes' misunderstanding of the text and not to any real contradiction in the Scriptures.

5. HARMONY WITH THE WHOLE – The text that most harmonizes with the vocabulary and style of the entire document and other possible writings of the author is preferred.

THE CANON

The word "canon" comes from the Greek word **kanôn**, which denotes a measuring rod, standard, or rule. In the Third Council of Carthage, this word was employed as a reference to the list of inspired books of the Scriptures that should be received as the standard or rule of Christian faith and conduct. The books that are inspired and included in the Bible are called "canonical." The books that are not inspired and are rejected from forming part of the sacred Scriptures are called "noncanonical."

THE OLD TESTAMENT CANON

The Old Testament Scriptures were written within a period of about one thousand years from 1450 to 400 B.C. The majority of conservative scholars (Jewish and Christian) believe that by 300 B.C. all the books of the Old Testament had been written, compiled, and recognized by the

Jewish people as Holy Scripture; the mere fact that the Old Testament Scriptures were translated into Greek between 280-150 B.C. (the Septuagint) supports such an early date. Some scholars believe, based on a strong Jewish tradition, that Ezra led the first council to recognize the books of the Jewish canon. It is important to note that Jesus and the apostles recognized the absolute authority of the Hebrew Scriptures.

THE NEW TESTAMENT CANON

The books of the New Testament canon were not determined by ecclesiastical councils or declarations, but by their acceptance among the churches and believers throughout the known world. At the end of the second century, the four Gospels, the book of Acts, and the thirteen epistles or letters of Paul had been widely received as sacred Scripture by believers and churches everywhere. By the time of the Third Council of Carthage in A.D. 397, all the books of the New Testament that had already been accepted by the churches at large were recognized as sacred Scripture.

To conclude this brief discussion of the New Testament canon, it will be helpful to consider how the churches, councils, and Church fathers decided which books should be included. To be received into the canon as part of the New Testament, a book had to meet certain requirements within the following areas.

Authorship: The author had to be an apostle or someone who was in the circle of their fellowship (such as Mark, Luke, or possibly the writer of Hebrews).

Content: The book's teaching or doctrine had to be in harmony with the other books of sacred Scripture.

Universal Acceptance: The book had to be recognized by the entire Church.

Acceptance by the Church Fathers: The opinion of those who studied at the feet of the apostles was crucial. Did they accept the book as apostolic? Did they quote from the book in their own writings?

Personal Edification: The book had to have the capacity to inspire, convince, and edify Christians in knowledge and devotion.

THE APOCRYPHA

THE APOCRYPHAL BOOKS

The word "apocryphal" comes from the Greek adjective **apókruphos**, which means, "hidden." With regard to the canon, the word refers to the fourteen books that were excluded from the Old and New Testament canons. It was not until the Council of Trent in 1546 that the Roman Catholic Church declared eleven apocryphal books as canonical.[3] The First Vatican Council confirmed this decision in 1826. The apocryphal books are: **I Esdras, II Esdras, Book of Tobit, Book of Judith, Additions to Esther** (or Rest of Esther), **Book of Wisdom** (or Wisdom of Solomon), **Book of Ecclesiasticus** (or Wisdom of Sirach), **Book of Baruch** (and Letter of Jeremiah), **Prayer of Azariah** (and Song of the Three Holy Children), **Story of Susanna, Bel and the Dragon, Prayer of Manasseh, I Maccabees,** and **II Maccabees.**

[3] All of the listed books except for I Esdras, II Esdras, and Prayer of Manasseh.

CANONICAL ISSUES WITH THE APOCRYPHA

Below are some of the most important reasons why the apocryphal books were not and should not be considered equal to the Scriptures as a rule of faith or conduct.

1. **The apocryphal writings were never included in the Hebrew canon.**

2. **The Jewish synagogue never considered the apocryphal writings to be inspired.**

3. **None of the apocryphal writings claim to have been inspired by God.** Certain authors of the apocryphal writings even deny that they are inspired.[4]

4. **The Jews never cited the apocryphal writings as inspired works.**

5. **Neither Jesus nor the apostles ever cited the apocryphal writings as inspired works.**

6. **The famous Jewish historian Josephus and the Jewish philosopher Philo did not recognize the apocryphal writings as inspired.**

7. **Jerome, the translator of the Latin Vulgate, declared the apocryphal writings to be uninspired.**

8. **Some of the apocryphal writings contain notable historical, geographical, and doctrinal errors.**

9. **The inferior quality of the apocryphal writings becomes obvious when compared to the books of Scripture.**

10. **None of the apocryphal writings are found in a list of canonical books composed during the first four centuries of the Church.** Even the Roman Catholic Church did not officially recognize the apocryphal writings until 1546 at the Council of Trent.

SUMMARY

Considering the great evidence against the apocryphal writings, it is best to adopt the opinion of the Westminster Confession of Faith (1643) and the London Baptist Confession (1689):

> "The books commonly called 'The Apocrypha,' not being of divine inspiration, are not part of the canon or rule of Scripture and are therefore of no authority to the Church of God, nor are they to be approved of or made use of any differently from other human writings."[5]

---

[4] Prologue of Ecclesiasticus; I Maccabees 4:46; 9:27; II Maccabees 15:38-39
[5] London Baptist Confession, Chapter 1.3

Chapter 11: The Purpose of the Bible

Part One: The Bible and the Christian's Spiritual Awakening

Having considered the absolute trustworthiness of the Bible, we will now turn our attention toward its great purpose in the Christian life. The following list includes nine key purposes of the Bible which we will study in this and the next two chapters: the Bible (1) reveals Jesus Christ and His salvation; (2) is the basis or foundation of our faith; (3) validates our beliefs; (4) promotes sanctification; (5) instructs in righteousness and wisdom; (6) gives hope and comfort; (7) gives strength in spiritual warfare; (8) brings blessing; and (9) brings life, joy, and praise.

THE BIBLE REVEALS JESUS CHRIST AND HIS SALVATION

Jesus of Nazareth is the most important person in history. He is the fulfillment of all the promises of God and the only hope for mankind. The destiny of every person depends upon his or her relationship with Him. Those who confess Jesus Christ as Lord and Savior will be saved. Those who deny Him will be eternally lost. He is found on nearly every page of the Bible, from its first words to its last chapter. In the Old Testament, He is the promised Savior. In the Gospels, He is the promise fulfilled, the Savior of the world, the Lord of glory, and the coming King. The Bible's most crucial purpose is to reveal Christ and the salvation that is mediated through Him. The goal of all our Bible study should be to know Christ, to comprehend His salvation and will, and to be conformed to His image.

1. According to John 5:39-40, what is the great purpose of the Scriptures?

_____

_____

_____

_____

2. According to the words of Philip in John 1:45, what is the main purpose and theme of the Old Testament?

_____

_____

_____

_____

NOTES: The phrase, "the Law and the Prophets," was employed in the time of Christ as a reference to the entire Old Testament. The revelation of Jesus Christ does not begin in the New Testament; rather, it is seen in the very first words of the Scriptures!

3. The Bible reveals not only the person of Jesus but also the salvation that can be found in Him alone. What do the following texts teach us about this truth?

   a. *John 20:30-31*

   _____

   _____

   _____

   _____

   b. *II Timothy 3:15*

   _____

   _____

   _____

   _____

4. The teaching found in the above texts is extremely important for the student of the Scriptures. The knowledge of mere facts and precepts is not the purpose of our study of God's Word; the purpose is the knowledge of Christ, "in whom are hidden all the treasures of wisdom and knowledge" (Colossians 2:3). The study of the Bible is more than an intellectual exercise; it is the search for a Person—God in Christ. What does Jeremiah 9:23-24 teach us about this truth?

   _____

   _____

_____

_____

_____

_____

THE BIBLE IS THE BASIS OF OUR FAITH

We are saved by faith (Ephesians 2:8), and without faith it is impossible to please God (Hebrews 11:6). But what is faith? Only the Bible gives us a clear answer to this crucial question.

1. How does the Bible define faith in Hebrews 11:1?

   a. *Faith is the A_____ of that for which we have H_____.*

   b. *Faith is the C_____ of what we have not S_____.*

   > **NOTES:** Hebrews 11:1 gives us one of the most important definitions of faith found in the entire Bible; however, to understand its full significance, we must answer two questions. **First**, how can we have assurance of our hope? **Answer:** We can have the assurance of that for which we hope because God has promised it in His Word. **Second**, how can we have the conviction of what we have never seen? **Answer:** We can have conviction of what we have not seen because God has promised it in His Word.

2. In Romans 4:18-21, the Bible give us a powerful illustration regarding the relationship between the Word of God and faith. Abraham was nearly a hundred years old, his wife Sarah was sterile, and they still had no children. But in spite of these circumstances, Abraham believed in the promise of God—he believed that he would have a son. According to Romans 4:21, what was the basis or foundation of his confidence?

   a. *Abraham was fully A_____ (that he would have a son) because God*

      had P_____.

   > **NOTES:** Abraham could not **see** his son who had not been born, and the circumstances discouraged hope. However, Abraham was assured that he would have a son because God promised it and was able to perform what He had promised! Abraham's faith was based upon the Word of God and the integrity of God's character. Here we learn a valuable lesson: *genuine faith is impossible apart from the knowledge of God's promises.*

3. Based on the Scriptures that we have studied, explain this truth: genuine faith is impossible apart from the knowledge of God's promises.

_____

_____

_____

_____

_____

_____

THE BIBLE VALIDATES OUR BELIEFS

We have learned that God has revealed Himself and His will through theophanies, visions, dreams, an audible voice, angels, and miracles. We also understand that God gave us the greatest revelation of Himself two thousand years ago through the incarnation of Jesus Christ. Yet, how does God speak to His people today? How can we know that what we have seen, heard, and felt is true? What is the authority by which we can test the validity of our beliefs and actions? The answer is found in the Bible.

1. What does II Timothy 3:16-17 teach about the Bible and its authority in the life of the Church and the individual Christian?

_____

_____

_____

_____

_____

_____

NOTES: The Bible is the highest authority in the Christian life. Any revelation, idea, teaching, experience, attitude, or action that does not conform to the Word of God must be rejected.

2. Isaiah 8:19-20 demonstrates the importance of making God's Word the standard to which we compare all other teachings. What does this text teach?

_____

_____

_____

_____

_____

3. In the church in Corinth, there were doctrinal and moral problems because the Christians were giving more attention to experiences than to the Word of God. To resolve the problems, what did the Apostle Paul command in I Corinthians 14:36-38?

_____

_____

_____

_____

4. We have learned that the Scriptures are the ultimate authority for all our beliefs and practices. According to Mark 7:7-9, 13, what was the great error of the Pharisees? Why did Jesus rebuke them so strongly?

_____

_____

_____

_____

NOTES: The Pharisees exalted their traditions over the Word of God and were led into serious error. However, we must be aware that there are many other things besides tradition that we can wrongly exalt over the Scriptures: our own ideas, the opinions of men, spiritual experiences, and more. We must be careful to submit all things to the scrutiny of God's Word. That which is not conformed to the Scriptures must be rejected.

5. According to II Timothy 2:15, what can we do to avoid the error or heresy of the Pharisees and the church in Corinth?

_____

_____

_____

_____

_____

Chapter 12: The Purpose of the Bible

Part Two: The Bible and the Christian's Spiritual Growth

In this chapter, we will continue our study of the purposes or goals of the Bible in the life of the Christian.

THE BIBLE PROMOTES SANCTIFICATION

God's greatest purpose in our lives is our sanctification—to conform us to the image of His Son (Romans 8:29). The word "sanctify" comes from the Latin word *sanctificare* (*sanctus* = holy + *facere* = to make), which means, "to set apart" and "to make holy." Sanctification is the process of spiritual growth through which we become less like this fallen world and more like Christ. In the following exercises, we will learn that the Bible is a key element in this process.

1. According to John 17:15-17, how does God sanctify His children?

_____

_____

_____

_____

2. In Romans 12:2, the Apostle Paul sets before us a prohibition, an exhortation, and the means to obey both. His statements demonstrate that the Scriptures are foundational to our sanctification.

   a. *The Prohibition: Do not be C_____ to this world.* Literally, do not be "made of the same mold" as this fallen and sinful world.

   b. *The Exhortation: Be T_____.* This exhortation comes from the Greek word *metamorphóō* and can be translated, "Be metamorphosed." It is the same word used by scientists to describe the transformation of a caterpillar into a butterfly. The word was also used by Matthew to describe the transformation of the Lord Jesus Christ on the Mount of Transfiguration (Matthew 17:1-2).

   c. *The Means: By the R_____ of your mind.* This renewal is achieved through internalizing the Word of God. Our freedom from the daily influence of sin and our progress toward maturity and conformity to Christ depend upon the saturation of our lives in the Scriptures.

3. In John 8:34, Jesus taught that the person who lives in sin is a slave to sin. According to verses 31-32, how can the Christian experience greater liberty from the power of sin and grow in sanctification?

_____

_____

_____

_____

NOTES: The word "continue" (v.31) comes from the Greek word **ménō**, which means, "to abide, remain, lodge, or take up residence." If we are to be free from sin and grow in conformity to Christ, we must "make our home" in the Word of God.

4. By abiding in the Word of God we can experience greater liberty from the tyranny of sin. This principle is illustrated well in Psalm 119:9-11. What can we learn from verses 9 and 11?

_____

_____

_____

_____

5. In Psalm 119:11, David declared, "Your word I have treasured in my heart, that I may not sin against You." In the following exercise, write the very **opposite** of what David declared to come to an even greater understanding of the need to saturate our lives in the Word of God.

   a. *"Your word I have **not** T_____ in my heart, that I **might** S_____ against You."*

   NOTES: The Christian who saturates his life in the Scriptures builds a fortress that protects him from the deadly influence of sin. The Christian who neglects the study of God's Word opens the door to sin and puts himself in danger.

THE BIBLE INSTRUCTS IN RIGHTEOUSNESS AND WISDOM

It can be said that the Bible is the manual for the Christian life. Without the Bible, it is impossible to fully obey God and live according to His plan for our lives. The instruction, wisdom, and discipline of the Scriptures are indispensable.

1. According to Proverbs 1:2-4, what are the benefits that the Bible promises to those who seek to learn from it?

   a. *W_____ (v.2)*. Knowledge and the proper use of it.

   b. *I_____ (v.2)*. Includes correction and discipline.

   c. *The ability to D_____ wise sayings or counsel (v.2)*.

   d. *I_____ in wise B_____, marked by righteousness, justice, and integrity (v.3)*.

   e. *P_____ (v.4)*. Includes sensibility, caution, and shrewdness.

   f. *K_____ (v.4)*. The right information.

   g. *D_____ (v.4)*. The ability to make proper decisions.

2. God's Word promises wisdom to all who endeavor to learn its truths, regardless of their apparent inability. According to Proverbs 1:4-5, who can grow in wisdom through the Scriptures?

   a. *The N_____ (v.4)*. The open-minded; those who are easily deceived because of their lack of judgment.

   b. *The Y_____ (v.4)*. Those who have experienced little of life or learning.

   c. *The W_____ and U_____ (v.5)*. Those who have already attained a high degree of knowledge, wisdom, and understanding.

   NOTES: Through the Scriptures, the knowledge and wisdom of God are within reach of all people. The young and naive can become wise, and the wise can grow wiser still.

3. According to Proverbs 1:7, what is the greatest ethical truth or moral wisdom that the Scriptures can impart to us? Explain your answer.

   _____

   _____

   _____

   _____

   NOTES: The word "fear" comes from the Hebrew word **yirah**, which can also be translated, "reverence" or "respect." With regard to God, it denotes the deepest reverence and respect leading to worship and obedience. The fear of the Lord is the foundation and first step of all true knowledge.

4. According to II Timothy 3:16, what are the four ways in which the Scriptures reveal God's will to us and transform us into the image of His Son?

   a. *Through T_____.* From the Greek word **didaskalía**, which denotes instruction, doctrine, or teaching. The Bible is the basis and source of all knowledge pertaining to salvation—doctrine, ethics, morality, character, wisdom, right thinking, right living, and so forth.

   b. *Through R_____.* From the Greek word **elégchō**, meaning, "rebuke," "reproach," or "reproof." As a prosecuting attorney reveals evidence against a defendant in order to have him convicted of a crime, the truths of Scripture also convict us of our wrongs. The Scriptures not only reveal **God** to us, but they also reveal **us** to us. Hebrews 4:12 declares: "For the word of God is living and active and sharper than any two-edged sword, and piercing as far as the division of soul and spirit, of both joints and marrow, and able to judge the thoughts and intentions of the heart."

   c. *Through C_____.* From the Greek word **epanórthōsis**, which refers to the restoration of something to its proper conditions. In secular Greek, it was used to describe the act of setting a fallen object upright or helping those who have fallen or stumbled back to their feet. The Bible is not just a prosecuting attorney that shows us our wrong; it is also a doctor and counselor to mend us and put us back on the right path.

   d. *Through T_____ in R_____.* The word "training" comes from the Greek word **paideía**, which refers to the training, education, or nurturing of a child. The Bible provides positive and practical instruction leading to application and changed behavior.

5. According to I Timothy 1:5, what is the goal of all true biblical instruction?

   _____

   _____

   _____

6. Based on Matthew 7:24-27, compare the man who builds his life upon the Word of God with the man who does not.

   _____

   _____

   _____

   _____

_____

_____

_____

_____

THE BIBLE GIVES HOPE AND COMFORT

Problems and trials do not disappear simply because we have become Christians. Jesus taught that in this world we would have tribulations (John 16:33). In difficult times, we need a sure hope and comfort. In the Bible are countless promises, each one designed to encourage us to follow God with confidence and without fear.

1. According to Romans 15:4, what is one of the great purposes for which the Scriptures were written?

_____

_____

_____

_____

2. In Psalm 119:49-56, we read of the trials that David suffered and how he responded to them. We can learn much from his example. Read the text until you are familiar with its contents, and then answer the following questions.

   a. *According to the following verses, what were the trials that David suffered?*

      (1) He suffered A_____ (v.50).

      (2) The arrogant D_____ him (v.51).

      (3) Burning I_____ had seized him (v.53).

   b. *According to the following verses, how did David respond to the trials?*

      (1) He did not T_____ aside from God's Word (v.51).

      (2) He R_____ God's ancient ordinances (v.52).

      (3) He K_____ God's law (v.55).

c. *According to the following verses, how did the Word of God sustain David in his afflictions and trials?*

(1) God's Word was his C_____ in his affliction (v.50).

(2) God's Word R_____ him (v.50).

(3) God's statutes were his S_____ (v.54).

3. Based on the truths we just examined from Psalm 119:49-56, write a summary of how the Christian should rely upon the Word of God in the midst of trials.

_____

_____

_____

_____

_____

THE BIBLE GIVES STRENGTH IN SPIRITUAL WARFARE

The Christian's citizenship is in heaven (Philippians 3:20-21), yet he lives in the world. The Bible teaches that the entire world is under the dominion of the devil (II Corinthians 4:4; I John 5:19), who constantly wages war against the Christian who lives for the glory of God and who does His will. To experience greater victory in the Christian life, we need a weapon to guide and strengthen us against the devil and His schemes. The Bible is that weapon!

1. According to Ephesians 6:12, who seeks to oppose the Christian in his daily walk with Christ? Against whom or what must the Christian struggle?

_____

_____

_____

_____

_____

NOTES: What do these terms mean? To whom or what do they refer? There are many interpretations and speculations, but only one limited interpretation is certain. The above reference is to the devil and the demons who constantly work in this world to hinder the work of God and destroy the Christian's testimony. It is interesting that the word "struggle" comes from the Greek word *pálē*, which refers to a wrestling match. The word "against" denotes a face-to-face conflict.

2. According to Ephesians 6:10-16, the believer must live in righteousness, faith, and preparedness. Furthermore, he must avail himself of all the spiritual weapons that the Lord has given him. One of the most important of these weapons is referenced in Ephesians 6:17 as "the sword of the Spirit." According to the verse, to what does this refer?

   a. *The W_____ of G_____*. How is the Word of God the sword of the Spirit? The word "sword" is translated from the Greek word *máchaira*, which refers to a Roman short sword or dagger. It was primarily used as a defensive weapon. The noun "word" comes from the Greek word *rhêma*, which means, "that which is spoken; a declaration, message, or word." The Scriptures are God-breathed (II Timothy 3:16), and every word "proceeds out of the mouth of God" (Matthew 4:4). The Scriptures were written by men who were moved or carried by the Spirit (II Peter 1:21), and they are His work. As believers, we are to wield the Word of God in the power of the Holy Spirit in our battle against our spiritual enemies. When we are attacked, we must respond with confidence in and obedience to the Word of God, as Christ did when He strove with the devil in the wilderness (Matthew 4:1-11).

3. According to Matthew 4:4, 7, 10, how did Jesus triumph over the temptations of the devil? How can we follow His example?

   _____

   _____

   _____

   _____

   _____

   _____

   _____

NOTES: It is crucial to understand that the Lord did not triumph over the devil merely by quoting God's Word, but by obeying it! Similarly, we should not merely quote the Scriptures when battling temptation; we must believe and obey them!

4. According to I John 2:14, why were the young men to whom John was writing able to overcome the evil one?

    a. *They were S_____ because the Word of God A_____ in them.* The word "abides" comes from the Greek word **ménō**, which means, "to abide, remain, lodge, or take up residence." The young men were strong because they made their home in the Word of God. They had internalized God's Word and were living in obedience to it. They depended upon the Word in the midst of temptation; we must learn to follow their example.

Chapter 13: The Purpose of the Bible

Part Three: The Bible and the Christian's Spiritual Benefits

In this chapter, we will continue our study of the purposes or goals of the Bible in the life of the Christian.

THE BIBLE BRINGS BLESSING

God has given the believer every spiritual blessing in Christ (Ephesians 1:3), but without the Scriptures, it is impossible to know what those blessings are. The Bible is like a mine of incalculable riches. If we diligently seek its truths, we will find abundant treasures of blessings for our lives. Throughout the history of the Church, many Christians have lived like impoverished beggars sitting on a million bars of gold! They have had infinite spiritual blessings at their disposal, but they have not obtained them because of their neglect and ignorance of the Word of God. We must avoid this error and dedicate ourselves to knowing, believing, and obeying the promises of God.

1. Psalm 1:1-4 contains one of the most beautiful illustrations of the blessings that come through the Scriptures. Read over the text until you are familiar with its contents, and then complete the following exercises.

   a. *In light of verse 2, describe the proper response to the Word of God.*

   _____

   _____

   _____

   _____

   b. *In light of verse 3, describe the man who makes the Scriptures his delight and meditates upon them day and night.*

   _____

   _____

   _____

   _____

c. *In light of verse 4, describe the man who neglects the Scriptures and lives far from their influence.*

_____

_____

_____

_____

_____

2. In Joshua 1:1-8, God promised to give Joshua success in all things that were according to His will. According to verses 7-8, what did God require of Joshua?

   a. *Be C_____ to do according to all the L_____ of God (v.7).*

   b. *Do not T_____ from the Law to the right or the left (v.7).*

   c. *Meditate upon the Law of God D_____ and N_____ (v.8).*

3. James 1:25 contains a promise similar to that of Joshua 1:7-8. What does this text teach us about the blessing of God's Word and about our responsibility?

   _____

   _____

   _____

   _____

4. According to Luke 11:27-28, what does the Lord Jesus Christ teach us about the proper response to the Word of God and the results that should follow?

   _____

   _____

   _____

   _____

THE BIBLE BRINGS LIFE, JOY, AND PRAISE

The Bible is the greatest and most important book in the history of humanity. From it we learn about the history of redemption, salvation through Christ, and the infinite blessings that God has for all who believe. Some who do not know or understand the Bible may view it as an enslaving book full of rules and prohibitions, but the very opposite is true! The Bible is the book that God has given us to encourage and guide us in a world that is filled with dangers. Those who have read, believed, and obeyed the Bible know that it is a fountain of life, joy, and praise!

1. Some people wrongly believe that the Bible is enslaving and burdensome, but what do the following Scriptures teach about the true nature and effect of God's Word in the lives of those who believe?

   a. *John 6:63*

   _____

   _____

   _____

   _____

   NOTES: The flesh refers to our fallen humanity, which is totally incapable of producing true life or spirituality within us. In contrast, Christ's words are "spirit" and "life." The Holy Spirit works efficaciously through the Word of God, producing spiritual life within those who hear and believe.

   b. *John 8:31-32, 34*

   _____

   _____

   _____

   _____

   NOTES: The word "continue" comes from the Greek word *ménō*, which means, "to abide, remain, lodge, or take up residence." True freedom comes from "taking up residence" in the Word of God, relying upon its promises, and obeying its commands.

c. I John 5:3

_____

_____

_____

_____

NOTES: The word "burdensome" comes from the Greek word **barús**, which may also be translated, "heavy" or "hard." It denotes that which is burdensome, oppressive, or grievous. The word is used by Jesus in Matthew 23:4 with regard to the tedious and oppressive traditions of the Pharisees: "They tie up heavy [**barús**] burdens and lay them on men's shoulders..."

2. In Matthew 11:28-30, what does Jesus say about His own teaching? Is it burdensome and enslaving, or is it life-giving and liberating? Explain your answer.

_____

_____

_____

_____

_____

_____

3. In Psalm 119:44-45, David makes a key statement that connects obedience and freedom. According to David, does obedience to God's Word restrict the believer's freedom or amplify it? Explain your answer.

_____

_____

_____

_____

_____

_____

4. How does David describe the Word of God in Psalm 19:7-11? According to verses 10-11, was it a useless drudgery for him or a delight? Explain your answer.

_____

_____

_____

_____

_____

_____

5. The Bible is not some dry literary work; it is powerful and life-giving! When it has its rightful place in our lives, it results in peace, joy, and praise—even in the midst of difficult trials and circumstances. What do the following texts teach us about this truth?

   a. _Jeremiah 15:16_

   _____

   _____

   _____

   b. _Psalm 119:162-165_

   _____

   _____

   _____

c. *Psalm 119:71-72*

_____

_____

_____

_____

6. The joy, delight, and praise that the Word of God produces in our lives do not depend upon the circumstances that surround us. What does David declare about this truth in Psalm 119:143? How can this truth be applied to our own lives?

_____

_____

_____

_____

_____

7. We will conclude this chapter with a very important reminder. The Bible does not bring us life, joy, and peace merely because it reveals to us the will of God; these benefits are brought because the Scriptures direct us to God's Son, in whom we find life! What did Jesus teach regarding this truth in John 5:39-40? How is this a warning to us all?

_____

_____

_____

_____

_____

Chapter 14: The Power of God's Word

Part One: Guidance and Wisdom

The Bible is more than a book; it is the inspired Word of God, powerful and effective to change our lives and transform us into the image of Jesus Christ. The Bible uses several metaphors to demonstrate how it can transform our lives. In this and the next two chapters, we will consider these word pictures and their meanings.

THE BIBLE IS LIKE A LAMP

Even though the Christian has been redeemed and is a new creation in Christ, he must still live in a dark and fallen world. The Word of God is the only trustworthy light or lamp that can guide the Christian through the innumerable dangers of this life.

1. What does Psalm 119:105 teach us about the Word of God? According to Psalm 119:106, how should this truth be applied to our lives?

_____

_____

_____

_____

_____

2. Proverbs 6:20-23 is a beautiful and powerful passage that also refers to the Scriptures as a lamp that guides. Read the text until you are familiar with its contents, and then answer the following questions.

   a. *How is the Word of God described in verse 23?*

   _____

   _____

   _____

b. *According to verses 20-21, how should the Christian respond to the Word of God so that it might truly be a lamp to his feet and a light to his path?*

_____

_____

_____

_____

NOTES: The commandment of the father and teaching of the mother are both references to the God's law. In Deuteronomy 6:1-9, parents are commanded to teach the God's law to their children.

c. *According to verses 22-23, what promises do the Scriptures give to the one who lives by the light of the Word?*

_____

_____

_____

_____

THE BIBLE IS LIKE A COUNSELOR

There are many voices in this corrupt and fallen world that constantly cry out for the Christian's attention, but the only counselor who never errs or lies is the Word of God. The Scriptures are the source from which we must draw counsel and the standard by which all other counsel must be judged. As the prophet Isaiah declared in Isaiah 8:20: "To the law and to the testimony! If they do not speak according to this word, it is because they have no dawn."

1. What does David declare about the Word of God in Psalm 119:24? What was David's relationship with the Word of God, and what was his attitude toward it?

_____

_____

_____

_____

_____

NOTES: The word "advisers" or "counselors" (KJV/NKJV/ESV) comes from the Hebrew word *etsah*, which denotes one who gives counsel, advice, strategy, or proper planning.

2. Psalm 119:97-104 is a powerful text that demonstrates the great blessings which result from making the Word our chief counselor. Read the text until you are familiar with its contents, and then answer the following questions.

   a. *According to verses 97 and 103, what was David's attitude toward the Word of God? What should our attitude be?*

   _____

   _____

   _____

   _____

   b. *According to verses 98-100, what was the blessing or advantage that David received by making the Word of God his counselor?*

   _____

   _____

   _____

   c. *It is not enough to simply listen to the counsel of God's Word; we must also obey it. According to verses 101-104, how was this truth reflected in David's life? How should it be reflected in ours?*

   _____

   _____

_____

_____

_____

3. Psalm 32:8-9 contains both a promise and an exhortation regarding God's counsel and our need to respond to it in obedience. Read the text until you are familiar with its contents, and then answer the following questions.

    a. *What does God promise to the believer in verse 8?*

    _____

    _____

    _____

    _____

    b. *What is God's exhortation to every believer in verse 9?*

    _____

    _____

    _____

    _____

4. We will conclude our consideration of God's Word as a counselor with one of the most beautiful promises found in the Scriptures regarding God's guidance. Write your thoughts on Psalm 73:24 in the space below.

    _____

    _____

    _____

    _____

Chapter 15: The Power of God's Word

Part Two: Revelation and Destruction

The Bible uses several metaphors to demonstrate how it can transform our lives. In this chapter, we will continue to consider these metaphors and their meanings.

THE BIBLE IS LIKE A SWORD AND A MIRROR

At first it may be difficult to see why these two metaphors should be considered together. Swords and mirrors do not seem to have much in common, yet in the context of Scripture they serve a similar purpose. The Word of God is like a sword or a surgeon's scalpel in that it opens and exposes the deepest part of our heart to reveal what is hiding inside. In a similar way, the Word of God is like a mirror in that it shows us our true reflection—who we really are.

1. In Hebrews 4:12-13, the Bible is presented as a sword that God uses to open and expose who we really are. Read through the text until you are familiar with its contents, and then answer the following questions.

   a. *Identify the three characteristics of the Word of God presented in verse 12.*

      (1) L_____. The Scriptures are God-breathed (II Timothy 3:16); they are both living and life-giving. The world was brought into existence and given life by His spoken word (Genesis 1). Jesus said that the words He spoke were "spirit" and "life" (John 6:63).

      (2) A_____. This comes from the Greek word **energês**, which may be translated, "active" or "effective." The Word is not dormant, passive, or inert. It **effectually works** in the life of the believer to expose his true self and conform him to the image of Christ.

      (3) S_____ than any two-edged sword. The Word of God has the power to break through our veneers and pretenses to expose our true self. It cuts through the heart of stone like a razor-sharp sword through butter in order to expose our most inward self.

   b. *According to verse 12, just how penetrating is the Word of God?*

   _____

   _____

   _____

   _____

_____

_____

NOTES: Three examples are taken from three realms of our existence: the spiritual (soul and spirit), the physical (joints and marrow), and the intellectual (thoughts and intentions). The writer's great purpose is to show that the Word of God is able to penetrate to the very core of our person and works, exposing the true character of all that we are and all that we do.

c. *In verse 13, the writer of Hebrews turns our attention to the God who inspired the Scriptures; he does this to prove the power of the Scriptures to penetrate and expose the very depths of our being and works. What important truths does he teach us?*

_____

_____

_____

_____

_____

_____

NOTES: God is omniscient. His knowledge of our innermost character, thoughts, and deeds is exhaustive. Furthermore, He works to rid us of wrong and conform us to the image of His Son. He has also inspired the Scriptures and uses them in our lives to give us the same true knowledge of ourselves so that we might reject the wrong that is revealed and labor with Him to be conformed to the image of His Son.

d. *Based on the truths we have learned from Hebrews 4:12-13, how should we respond? Should we give more time to the study of God's Word? Should we examine ourselves with greater care when we study the Scriptures? Write your thoughts; it will also be helpful to consider Lamentations 3:40-41.*

_____

_____

_____

_____

_____

2. James 1:22-25 is one of the most important texts in the Scriptures regarding the Bible's power to reveal our true self or character. Answer the following questions regarding this passage.

   a. *According to verse 23, what is one of the key functions of the Scriptures?*

      (1) The Scriptures are like a M_____ that shows a man the true character of his face. As the believer reads, studies, and meditates upon God's Word, it works as a mirror to reflect his true character and the integrity of all his works.

   b. *In verses 22 and 25, James separates those who study the Bible into two very different categories. What are these two categories?*

      (1) D_____ of the Word (v.22); E_____ doers (v.25). The Greek phrase "effectual doer" (**poiētês érgou**) may be translated literally as, a "doer of work" or a "doer who acts" (ESV), emphasizing an active or working response to what one has heard or learned. This describes the person who, through the hearing of God's Word, increases his knowledge of God's will and of his own deficiencies and then acts upon what he has learned, striving to conform his character and deeds to the will of God.

      (2) H_____ who delude themselves (v.22); F_____ hearers (v.25). This describes the person who hears and then quickly forgets. After taking a quick glance at his own reflection in the Word of God, he does nothing to seek greater conformity to Christ, because he is either blind to his revealed faults or simply does not care enough to expend the necessary energy to remedy them.

   c. *According to verses 22 and 25, what are the outcomes for the doer who acts and for the hearer who does nothing?*

      (1) The doers are B_____ in what they do. This description should remind us of the man of Psalm 1:1-3 who delights in the law of the Lord: "He will be like a tree firmly planted by streams of water, which yields its fruit in its season and its leaf does not wither; and in whatever he does, he prospers" (v.3).

      (2) The hearers who forget D_____ themselves. The word comes from the Greek word **paralogízomai**, which means, "to reason falsely, miscalculate, or deceive" or "to deceive by false arguments or reasoning." What the Word of God says about us is true. It is foolish to argue against its verdicts, to make excuses for ourselves in response to its reproofs, or to ignore the truth that it has shown us.

3. Based on what we have learned from Hebrews 4:12-13 and James 1:22-25, write a summary of how the wise man will respond to God's Word.

_____

_____

_____

_____

_____

_____

_____

THE BIBLE IS LIKE A HAMMER AND LIKE FIRE

When we consider the many virtues of the Word of God, we tend to focus on its power to create, instruct, and edify. For this reason, it may be somewhat difficult to view the Scriptures as an instrument to break, tear down, and destroy. Nevertheless, if we are committed to the self-testimony of Scripture, we must recognize that this is another crucial aspect of its ministry to the believer.

1. How does the prophet Jeremiah describe the Word of God in Jeremiah 23:29?

    a. *The Word is like a H_____ which S_____ a rock.* Nothing can stand between the Word of God and its fulfillment according to the sovereign purposes of God. It has the power to break open hearts of stone, destroy sin, and demolish every error that opposes the truth of God. In this same text, God also uses the metaphor of a consuming fire. In both cases, the idea is that God's Word not only renews and edifies but also destroys and consumes.

2. In Jeremiah 1:4-10 we read of Jeremiah's calling into the prophetic office. According to verse 10, what was the purpose of Jeremiah's message? How can this apply to the ministry of the Word of God in our own lives?

_____

_____

NOTES: In this text we see that before God can build up, He must also pluck up, break down, destroy, and overthrow many things in our lives that are not in accordance with His will. At times, God will use His Word to carry out this painful but essential work.

3. In II Corinthians 10:4-5, the Apostle Paul describes one aspect of his ministry that appears very similar to that of Jeremiah in Jeremiah 1:10. According to this text, what are some ways in which the Word of God and prayer may be employed like a hammer?

   a. *They are likened to W_____ of W_____ (v.4).* The Christian life is a spiritual battle that cannot be waged by fleshly means such as eloquence, deception, or clever strategies. Only the divinely ordained and empowered means of the Word of God and prayer are sufficient.

   b. *For the D_____ of F_____ (v.4).* The word "destruction" comes from the Greek word **kathaíresis**, which may also be translated, "tearing down" or "pulling down." The idea is similar to that found in Jeremiah 1:10. The word "fortresses" comes from the Greek word **ochúrōma**, denoting a fort or stronghold. There are often many strongholds of sin that must be destroyed in our lives before we can advance in sanctification and become abundantly fruitful. The Word of God and prayer are powerful means to carry out this task.

   c. *For D_____ S_____ (v.5).* The word "destroying" (**kathairéō**) comes from the same root as "destruction" in verse 4 and carries the same meaning. The word "speculations" comes from the Greek work **logismós**, which in this context refers to carnal speculations or reasoning—ideas that are not conformed to the true knowledge and will of God. Such speculations can only be destroyed through the proper use of the Word of God.

   d. *For destroying E_____ L_____ thing raised up against the knowledge of God (v.5).* The Bible is not opposed to lofty or high thoughts; rather, it encourages men to make full use of their minds and gifts of reason. However, the Scriptures do oppose every so-called lofty thought or doctrine that exalts itself above the true knowledge of God and contradicts His revealed will. Again, only the Scriptures are sufficient for exposing and pulling down such error.

e. *For taking every thought C_____ to the O_____ of Christ (v.5).* Jesus Christ is Lord, and His will is the highest of all law. The goal of our faith is perfect obedience to Christ. To bring every thought, word, and deed into subjection to the will of Christ requires that we know God's Word and be empowered by it.

4. In our study, we have learned that it is at times necessary to tear down and destroy the sins and erroneous ideas in our lives before we can be rebuilt according to the will of God. It is a difficult and sometimes unpleasant experience, but it is absolutely necessary if we are to be conformed to the image of Christ. In II Timothy 4:2-4, the Apostle Paul gives sound advice regarding this truth. In verse 2, he writes that God's Word not only teaches us but also reproves, rebukes, and exhorts us. Then, in verses 3-4, he warns of a dangerous error that many will commit. What is this error, and how can we avoid it?

_____

_____

_____

_____

_____

_____

_____

Chapter 16: The Power of God's Word

Part Three: Sustenance and Fruitfulness

The Bible uses several metaphors to demonstrate how it can transform our lives. In this chapter, as in the previous two, we will consider some of these metaphors and their meanings.

THE BIBLE IS LIKE MILK AND LIKE SOLID FOOD

Both the most mature believer and the most recent convert have need of proper nourishment in order to be spiritually healthy and to grow in grace. This "spiritual food" is found in the Word of God.

1. What did the Lord Jesus Christ teach in Matthew 4:4 with regard to the relationship that exists between every believer and the Word of God?

_____

_____

_____

_____

NOTES: Jesus is neither minimizing the importance of food nor promoting an ascetic (*i.e.* rigorously self-denying) lifestyle. Rather, His words must be interpreted in light of the essentiality of food and proper nutrition. His logic is clear and powerful. Food is absolutely essential to human life—much the same as water and oxygen. We cannot sustain physical life apart from physical food. In the same way, the Word of God is absolutely essential to all spiritual life. If it is absurd to think that a man can live without food, it is equally absurd to think that a Christian can live without the Word of God.

2. The truth that Jesus taught in Matthew 4:4 is wonderfully displayed in the attitude of Job in Job 23:12. What was Job's attitude toward the Word of God, and how can we imitate him in this?

_____

_____

_____

_____

_____

3. Some erroneously believe that the Scriptures are only for pastors and for believers who are unusually gifted or advanced in the faith. This, however, could not be further from the truth! How can a new Christian ever grow to maturity unless he receives the nutrition he needs from the Scriptures? What exhortation does the Apostle Peter give to young believers in I Peter 2:2? How should his exhortation be applied to our daily lives?

_____

_____

_____

_____

_____

_____

4. Milk provides excellent nutrition for babies, but no child can grow to maturity by drinking milk alone—he must also learn to eat solid food. There are many in the Church who are content with only the most fundamental teachings of the Scriptures; they do not press on to understand the depths of God's revealed truth or the greater demands of His will. Therefore, their discernment and commitment to the Lord remains at the level of a child. In many ways, the church in Corinth is an example of such spiritual immaturity. Read through I Corinthians 3:1-3 until you are familiar with its contents, and then answer the following questions.

   a. _What is the overall opinion of the Apostle Paul regarding the believers in I Corinthians 3:1-3?_

_____

_____

_____

_____

b. *Based on the texts we have already considered, what would have been the best remedy for the spiritual immaturity of the believers in Corinth? How could you apply the same remedy to your own life?*

_____

_____

_____

_____

_____

5. In Hebrews 5:11-14 we find the same spiritual immaturity that was in the church in Corinth. Read through the text until you are familiar with its contents, and then answer the following questions.

a. *In verses 11-13, how does the writer describe the Christian who is still an infant in his knowledge and use of the Word of God?*

_____

_____

_____

_____

_____

b. *In verse 14, how does the writer describe the mature believer and his relationship with the Word of God?*

_____

_____

_____

_____

c. *How can the truths that we have gleaned from Hebrews 5:11-14 be applied to our own lives?*

_____

_____

_____

_____

_____

6. In II Timothy 2:15, what exhortation does the Apostle Paul give to his young disciple Timothy so that he might be mature in his knowledge and use of the Word of God? How can we apply this same exhortation to our own lives?

_____

_____

_____

_____

THE BIBLE IS LIKE SEED AND RAIN

Two of the most powerful metaphors employed in the Scriptures to communicate the eminence and power of the Word of God in the Christian life are "seed" and "rain." As a plant cannot exist apart from seed and cannot grow to fruitfulness apart from rain, the Christian's life and growth to maturity and fruitfulness depend upon the Word of God.

1. Read through I Peter 1:23-25 until you are familiar with its contents, and then answer the following questions.

a. *According to verse 23, what is the seed through which the Spirit of God accomplishes His miraculous work of regeneration in our hearts? What is the means by which we are born again? What is the significance of this truth?*

_____

_____

_____

_____

_____

_____

NOTES: We were not born again through the wisdom of men or their clever arguments, but by the powerful Word of God, implanted as a seed in our hearts by the Spirit of God.

b. *How is the Word of God described in verses 23-25? How is this description an encouragement to the Christian?*

_____

_____

_____

_____

_____

_____

_____

NOTES: The Word of God is active (*i.e.* effectually working), accomplishing God's purposes in the heart of every Christian. It is also enduring—it will never diminish in its power or cease its work in us until it has accomplished its purpose.

2. The Parable of the Sower is one of the most important of Jesus' parables, as it demonstrates both the power of God's Word to change our lives and our responsibility to respond correctly to it. Read through Luke 8:4-15 until you are familiar with its contents, and then answer the following questions.

a. *According to verse 11, what is the seed that is sown?*

_____

_____

_____

_____

> **NOTES:** The "Word of God" denotes the word that proceeds out of the mouth of God (Matthew 4:4) and the word that is about God. It encompasses both the gospel, through which man enters the kingdom of heaven, and the full counsel of the Scriptures, through which he grows to maturity. The Word of God is the necessary element in all stages of the Christian life.

b. *According to verse 8 and Matthew 13:23, how great a harvest can the Word of God produce in our lives?*

_____

_____

_____

_____

> **NOTES:** The truth to be gained here is that every Christian who faithfully receives and abides in the Word of God has the promise of a life of abundant fruitfulness. Even the least among us has the promise of bearing fruit that is thirtyfold. It should be noted that there is also a serious warning here to those who claim to be Christians but bear no fruit. Even though the most dedicated Christian may pass through times of apparent fruitlessness, a life of barrenness is evidence that a person is not truly converted.

c. *Even though the Word of God is powerful, the parable of the sower demonstrates that its effectiveness within a believer is dependent upon the condition of his or her heart. According to verses 12-14, what are some of the factors that can limit the work of God's Word in our lives?*

(1) The D_____ (v.12). The devil is the enemy of God and man. He constantly labors to hinder the work of God's Word in our hearts. However, the point of verse 12 is not to highlight the devil's work but to highlight the responsibility of those who hear the Word of God. The devil can only "take away" the Word of God from a person's heart when that person's heart is hardened or unreceptive to the Word, like a hard road or trodden path that the seed cannot permeate.

(2) T_____ (v.13). Another factor that may limit the work of God's Word in a person's heart is temptation. This word comes from the Greek word **peirasmós**, denoting a trial, testing, or temptation. The Scriptures recognize that temptations

are a reality in this life, but they should not be used as an excuse for our behavior. If a person falls away from the Christian faith, it is because he received the Word only superficially—it never truly took root in his heart.

    (3) W_____, R_____, and P_____ of this life (v.14). Although God is sovereign and His Word is powerful, the outcome of our lives is also affected by the decisions we make. Many have allowed the Word of God to be choked out of their lives by the concerns and pleasures of this world. Too many people have traded eternal life for the temporal pleasures and concerns of this life.

d. *How does Luke 8:15 describe the heart in which the Word of God can produce fruit a hundredfold?*

_____

_____

_____

_____

_____

NOTES: Recognizing the sinful and morally depraved condition of every man's heart, it is obvious that anyone's willingness to truly receive the Word of God is the result of a previous work of God's grace.

3. Isaiah 55:10-11 presents one of the most beautiful descriptions of the Word of God. Explain this text in your own words. What do these truths mean for our lives?

_____

_____

_____

_____

_____

_____

_____

NOTES: The Word of God is not only like a living seed but also like a life-giving rain. Every purpose that God has for our lives can be fulfilled through the Word of God. If we sincerely receive the Word of God, it will transform our lives.

4. Deuteronomy 32:1-43 is called "The Song of Moses." In verse 2, Moses prayed that his proclamation of the Word of God might have an impact on the lives of God's people. How can we pray this same prayer for ourselves, that God's Word might impact us? Use the verse to fill in the blanks below.

   a. *Lord, let Your* T_____ *drop as the* R_____ *upon us.*

   Let your S_____ *distill or drip like the* D_____ *upon us, as the*

   D_____ *on the fresh* G_____.

5. Hebrews 6:7-8 contains a strong warning regarding a person's responsibility to respond correctly to the Word of God. It is very similar to the warnings in the Parable of the Sower. What is the warning, and how should it be applied to our lives?

   _____

   _____

   _____

   _____

   _____

   _____

NOTES: Even the most devoted Christian will sometimes struggle with apathy toward the Word and pass through times of apparent unfruitfulness. However, the person whose life is marked by constant unfruitfulness and even rebellion to the Word of God must consider the painful truth that he or she may not be truly converted.

Chapter 17: A Proper Attitude Toward God's Word

Part One: Study and Love the Word

The Bible is the inspired Word of God, indispensable for salvation and the Christian life. Other than the gift of Himself, the Bible is the greatest gift that God has given to the Christian. What should our attitude be toward this indescribable gift? In this chapter and the next, we will attempt to answer this question.

THE CHRISTIAN SHOULD CONSIDER THE BIBLE ACCESSIBLE

Many Christians do not study the Bible because they think that it is not within their reach or that it is too difficult for the "common" believer. This attitude is tragic, damaging, and directly contradictory to the Bible itself! The Scriptures were given to the entire Church, and God has given every believer the capacity to understand their truths and live in light of them.

1. What does I Peter 2:9 teach about every Christian, from the most trained scholar to the most recent convert or "babe" in Christ?

_____

_____

_____

_____

NOTES: The priesthood of every Christian is one of the most important doctrines in the Bible. Each Christian is a priest of God with the same privileges of knowing God and ministering in His name. The Bible is not solely for pastors and theologians; it is for all Christians. We can know God and His Word; furthermore, He has also given us the ability to proclaim His excellencies to others.

2. What does I Corinthians 2:14 teach about the natural man (*i.e.* the unconverted) and his relationship with the Word of God?

_____

_____

_____

_____

_____

> **NOTES:** The phrase "spiritually appraised" may also be translated, "spiritually discerned." To discern or understand the truths of Scripture, a person must be illuminated or guided by the Holy Spirit.

3. I Corinthians 2:14 teaches us that even the most intelligent man cannot truly understand the Word of God if he is unconverted. In contrast, what do the following Scriptures teach us about the believer's relationship with the Word of God?

    a. *I Corinthians 2:12*

_____

_____

_____

_____

_____

> **NOTES:** The personal pronoun "we" demonstrates that the Apostle Paul is directing this promise to believers like himself.

    b. *I John 5:20*

_____

_____

_____

_____

> **NOTES:** Christ revealed God to man through His incarnation (John 1:18), but He also continues to give light and understanding to all Christians through the ministry of the Holy Spirit.

c. *I John 2:27*

_____

_____

_____

_____

NOTES: "Anointing" comes from the Greek word ***chrísma***, which refers to the Holy Spirit. The phrase, "you have not need for anyone to teach you," must be understood in its context. The Apostle John is possibly combating the lie of false teachers that "common" believers could not understand the truth of God without their guidance. John was affirming that all believers have the greatest of all teachers—the Holy Spirit. He was not denying the clear teaching of the Scriptures that God has given ministers to the Church who are specially gifted in knowledge and teaching (Ephesians 4:11-12).

4. What promises do we find in the following Scriptures that encourage us to study the Word of God with confidence and joy?

a. *Deuteronomy 29:29*

_____

_____

_____

_____

NOTES: Some crucial truths are found here that we must not ignore. First, there are some mysteries that God reserves for Himself; we must walk in humility before Him and trust in Him even when we do not understand. Secondly, the truths that God does reveal to us are not only for our contemplation but also for our obedience.

b. *Deuteronomy 30:11-14*

_____

_____

_____

_____

_____

NOTES: Although there are extremely profound truths within the Scriptures that are difficult to understand, the greater part of the Bible can be grasped and obeyed by the most recent convert.

c. *Proverbs 2:3-6*

_____

_____

_____

_____

_____

5. In Acts 17:10-11, we are given a wonderful example of how believers of every level of maturity should respond to the Scriptures. What great truth do we learn from the Bereans? How should we imitate them?

_____

_____

_____

_____

THE CHRISTIAN SHOULD LOVE THE BIBLE AND HOLD IT IN THE HIGHEST REGARD

The Bible is not a dry book of impersonal rules and burdensome commands; it is a testimony of the love and faithfulness of God toward His people. In the Scriptures, we find the love and grace of God that saves us and the wisdom of God that teaches us how to live. The Christian who studies and applies the Scriptures will learn to love and appreciate this Book of books that brings immeasurable blessing.

A PROPER ATTITUDE TOWARD GOD'S WORD

1. In the Psalms of David, we see the great love and high regard that the king of Israel held in his heart for the Word of God. Explain how each of these texts should be reflected in the life of every Christian.

   a. *Psalm 119:47-48*

   _____

   _____

   _____

   _____

   b. *Psalm 119:127-131*

   _____

   _____

   _____

   _____

   c. *Psalm 119:14, 72, 162*

   _____

   _____

   _____

   _____

   d. *Psalm 56:4*

   _____

   _____

   _____

   _____

NOTES: This is an astounding text. David's praises of God's Word demonstrate its exalted place in his heart. The Scriptures are not independent of God; they proceed out of His mouth (Matthew 4:4) and bear His impeccable attributes.

2. According to the following verses from Psalm 119, how did David demonstrate that his love and high regard for God's Word was sincere? How should every believer imitate David in showing the same sincerity?

a. *Meditation (Psalm 119:97)*

_____

_____

_____

_____

b. *Obedience (Psalm 119:167)*

_____

_____

_____

_____

c. *Zeal (Psalm 119:136, 139)*

_____

_____

_____

_____

3. In Mark 4:23-25, the Lord Jesus Christ gives us a very important admonition and warning regarding the need to appreciate and respond correctly to the Word of God. Summarize His words, and apply them to your own life.

_____

_____

_____

_____

_____

NOTES: As we value God's Word and devote ourselves to it, more insight will be given to us. As we neglect God's Word, even the insight we possess will be taken away.

4. Do you have the same attitude as David toward the Word of God? Do you have a similar zeal? How do your love and high regard for the Scriptures manifest themselves in your daily life? Is there need for repentance? Write your thoughts.

_____

_____

_____

_____

_____

_____

Chapter 18: A Proper Attitude Toward God's Word

Part Two: Reverence and Respect the Word

In this chapter, we will continue our study of the proper attitude that every Christian should have regarding the Word of God.

THE CHRISTIAN SHOULD REVERENCE THE BIBLE

The Bible is the book that God has given to us so that we might know Him and obey His will. It is not the word of a man, but the Word of God (I Thessalonians 2:13); therefore, each word is worthy of reverence and obedience. The Bible is not a trivial or vain thing; rather, it is our very life (Deuteronomy 32:47)! For this reason, the Scriptures should instill a sense of awe and even fear within us.

1. The Scriptures teach us that the fear (or reverence) of the Lord and of His name is one of the most important aspects of our relationship with Him. According to Psalm 138:2, what has the Lord exalted with His name? What does this teach us about our relationship with the Scriptures? If we reverence the Lord's name, should we reverence His Word?

_____

_____

_____

_____

NOTES: "You have magnified Your word together with all Your name" (NASB - alternative reading). "You have magnified Your word above all Your name" (NKJV). "You have exalted above all things Your name and Your word" (ESV).

2. If we fear or reverence the Lord, we will also fear His Word that He has magnified with His name. What does Psalm 119:161 teach regarding the proper fear or reverence that the Christian should have toward the Word of God?

_____

_____

_____

_____

NOTES: The word "awe" comes from the Hebrew word **pachad**, which may also be translated, "fear" or "dread." David did not fear the most powerful men in the land, but he did stand in awe of God's Word.

3. The Bible teaches us that the fear of the Lord is an attitude of reverence toward God that will result in great moral changes in our lives. Those who fear God will also fear His Word and live in obedience to it. According to Deuteronomy 10:12-13, describe the lifestyle of those who truly live in the fear of the Lord and His Word.

_____

_____

_____

_____

4. According to Isaiah 66:2, what does God promise to those who fear or show reverence toward His Word?

_____

_____

_____

NOTES: The phrase, "to this one I will look," is a promise of God's special concern, fellowship, and blessing.

5. Reverence toward God and His Word is foundational to the Christian life. How does your relationship with the Scriptures reflect your reverence toward them? Is there a need for repentance in this area of your life? Write your thoughts.

_____

_____

_____

_____

_____

THE CHRISTIAN SHOULD CONSIDER THE SCRIPTURES ABSOLUTELY ESSENTIAL

The above statement may seem unnecessary or superfluous, as every true Christian clearly recognizes that the Scriptures are essential. However, how many Christians actually live out this truth in their daily lives? How many study the Bible as though their lives depend upon it? It is not a mystery why some Christians seem to walk with an unusual strength and wisdom, while others seem weak and wandering. The former have made the Scriptures their essential food and constant teacher, while the others have neglected the Word of God to their harm.

1. One of our greatest physical needs as humans is food. A person cannot survive without food, and there are many whose physical and mental development is seriously hindered because of their lack of proper nutrients. According to Matthew 4:4, how can this same principle be applied to a person's spiritual life?

_____

_____

_____

_____

2. What does Deuteronomy 32:46-47 teach about the paramount (*i.e.* of the highest importance) nature of the Word of God in the life of every Christian?

_____

_____

_____

_____

NOTES: The truth to be taken away from this passage is that our lives are totally and utterly dependent upon the great truths revealed in God's Word. It is impossible to overemphasize this truth.

3. The following are two of the most beautiful and powerful texts regarding the absolute essentiality of the Scriptures in the life of every believer. For each text, identify the blessings that are promised and the responsibility that is required.

   a. *Joshua 1:7-8*

   _____

   _____

   _____

   _____

   b. *Psalm 1:1-3*

   _____

   _____

   _____

   _____

4. Based on everything that we have learned in this chapter and the previous one, explain why the Scriptures are absolutely essential if the Christian is to grow to maturity in his faith and to walk in the power and wisdom of God.

   _____

   _____

   _____

   _____

   _____

   _____

   _____

Chapter 19: The Holy Spirit and the Scriptures

The Bible is a spiritual book. It was written by the Holy Spirit and can be interpreted only through His illumination and direction. Therefore, our relationship and communion with Him in prayer is an important factor in our ability to interpret the Scriptures. In fact, we simply cannot interpret the Bible correctly apart from prayer and the illuminating work of the Holy Spirit.

INSPIRATION AND ILLUMINATION

Before continuing our study, it is important to understand two key words or concepts that describe the relationship between the Holy Spirit and the Scriptures. These two concepts, defined below, are *inspiration* and *illumination*.

> **The Inspiration of the Holy Spirit:** The supernatural influence of the Holy Spirit upon the writers of the Scriptures that resulted in the completely infallible and trustworthy record of God's revelation.

> **The Illumination of the Holy Spirit:** The supernatural work of the Holy Spirit upon the readers of the Scriptures through which He teaches the Christian who sincerely searches for the truth and for the will of God in His Word.

Through the illumination of the Holy Spirit, God opens the Scriptures to the believer and teaches him its glorious truths. ***As the writing of the Bible would have been impossible apart from the inspiration of the Holy Spirit, so also the interpretation of the Bible is impossible apart from His illumination.*** These two ministries of the Spirit are absolutely essential, and it is necessary that we clearly understand the difference between the two.

1. **Illumination is not inspiration.** The inspiration of the Holy Spirit guaranteed the perfect transmission of the will of God through the writers of the Scriptures. The illumination of the Holy Spirit, although essential to our understanding of God's Word, does not guarantee that our interpretations will always be correct. There are other factors that can impede our understanding, such as pride, hardness of heart, false convictions, or distorted presumptions.

2. **The Holy Spirit will never teach anything that is not conformed to the grammar of the Word of God that He inspired.** Even though a verse can have many different *applications* for the Christian life, it has only one correct *interpretation*—that which is according to the grammatical and contextual meaning. If we interpret a text in a way that contradicts or adds to what is revealed in its wording, we have committed a grave and dangerous error.

3. **The illuminating work of the Holy Spirit does not nullify the need for teachers, preachers, Bible institutes, or seminaries.** In Romans 12:7 and Ephesians 4:11, the Scriptures clearly teach that the Lord has given the gift of teaching to some members of the Church, that they might be instruments through which the Holy Spirit instructs the Church.

ILLUMINATION OF THE HOLY SPIRIT IN THE SCRIPTURES

We must always remember the differences between the inspiration of the Scriptures and illumination. The illumination of the Holy Spirit does not guarantee that everything we interpret in the Bible will be correct. Many Christians, even leaders, have strayed from biblical doctrine by following the supposed illumination of the Holy Spirit without submitting themselves to the grammar of the Scriptures that the Holy Spirit Himself wrote. Illumination does not mean that the Spirit will guide us through some voice or feeling in the heart, but that He will teach us through what He has written in the Scriptures.

1. John 14:26 and John 16:13-15 are often quoted with reference to the illuminating work of the Holy Spirit. Although they do have a general and limited application to all believers, Christ is primarily referring to the work of the Holy Spirit in inspiring the apostles to write the New Testament. There are other texts of Scripture, however, that do refer to the doctrine of illumination and that clearly apply to all believers everywhere and at all times. The most important of these are listed below. Explain their meaning and application for every Christian.

   a. *Romans 8:14*

   _____

   _____

   _____

   _____

   _____

   NOTES: The phrase "being led" is in the present tense, indicating continuous action. The Spirit of God is faithful to lead the Christian, especially when he is diligent to study God's Word.

   b. *I Corinthians 2:9-10*

   _____

   _____

   _____

   _____

_____

_____

NOTES: The spiritual realities, which the natural or unconverted man cannot understand, are revealed to the believer through the Holy Spirit. This promise becomes even more tangible the more we devote ourselves to searching out these spiritual realities in the Scriptures.

c. *I Corinthians 2:12*

_____

_____

_____

_____

_____

d. *I John 2:27*

_____

_____

_____

_____

_____

NOTES: The word "anointing" comes from the Greek word ***chrísma***. In this context, the word refers to the Person of the Holy Spirit. This text does not deny the need for teachers and preachers (see Romans 12:7 and Ephesians 4:11-12). It simply affirms that every believer is able to understand the great truths of the Scriptures through the illuminating work of the Holy Spirit.

2. We have learned that the Holy Spirit has been given to lead us into the amazing truths of Scripture. However, according to the following texts, how can we limit or restrict the illuminating work of the Spirit within us? Match each danger with its corresponding text.

_____ Matthew 13:15

a. By wanting to hear only those truths that tickle our ears (i.e. please our flesh and cause it no discomfort).

_____ Acts 7:51

b. By quickly forgetting the truths that we have learned and not putting them into practice.

_____ I Thessalonians 5:19-20

c. By resisting the Holy Spirit's leadership through the truths of Scripture.

_____ II Timothy 4:3

d. By desiring only the milk or basic teachings of the Word and rejecting the greater and more demanding teachings that lead to maturity.

_____ Hebrews 5:13-14

e. By purposefully closing our eyes and ears to biblical truths that we do not want to hear.

_____ James 1:22-25

f. By despising or regarding with contempt the truths that are communicated to us through the proclamation of the Word or through personal study.

3. The Scriptures above show us that we must be careful not to hinder or restrict the Spirit's illuminating work in our lives. According to the following Scriptures, what can we do to work with the Spirit and grow in our knowledge of God? Match each action with its corresponding text.

_____ John 7:17

a. We must be diligent to study the Scriptures. God has decreed the Bible to be the means through which we grow in our knowledge of His person and will.

_____ Mark 4:24-25

b. We must be willing to obey the truth that we hope to find. Why should the Spirit teach truth to someone who is not willing to obey it?

_____ II Timothy 2:15

c. We must be willing to practice what we learn and teach it to others. The truth is meant to be shared with others.

_____ Ezra 7:10

d. We must have a high regard for God's truth and respond appropriately to the truth we do know. Why should God give us more truth if we will not obey the truth we already have?

Chapter 20: Prayer and the Scriptures

We learned in the previous chapter that, without God's help, we cannot understand the Scriptures or correctly apply them to our lives. Our intellect alone cannot grasp the things of God, and our hearts are not always open or sensitive to His will. For these reasons, we need the Holy Spirit to illuminate the Word, open our hearts, and teach us the truth. We are the students, the Bible is the text, and the Spirit of God is the Teacher in whom we may have full confidence and upon whom we must depend.

It is in this relationship of absolute dependence that we discover the vital importance of prayer. We must not simply presume upon God's help to understand the Scriptures; we must cry out to Him in faith and then follow His leadership. Below, we will study the essential relationship between prayer and the interpretation of God's Word.

1. It is true that many Christians struggle in their attempts to study the Word of God, often leading them to abandon their studies. They find the Scriptures difficult to understand, or their reading and study seems dry and lacking in real blessing. They become convinced that the study of the Scriptures is only for the pastor in the church or the theologian in the seminary. They do not recognize that their failure may be pointing them to a missing element in their study time—prayer! What does James 4:2 teach us regarding this truth?

    a. *You do not H_____ because you do not A_____.*

    > **NOTES:** Even though the immediate context of this verse has to do with material blessing, the wider application relates to every need of the believer. If we are struggling to understand the truths of God's Word and apply them to our lives, we are admonished to ask the Lord, who is gracious to His people and desires that they understand His person, His works, and His will.

2. A lack of prayer in our study of the Scriptures can be evidence of a self-sufficient attitude—that we believe ourselves to be capable of understanding the Scriptures without the help of its Author. To bring us back to reality, we only need to ask ourselves, "How can a finite man understand an unfathomable Book written by an infinite Author?" We must recognize our great need of God and turn to Him in prayer. What does James 1:5 promise to all Christians who find themselves in need of God's help to understand His will? How should we live in light of this truth?

    _____

    _____

    _____

_____

_____

3. In James 1:5, God promises to give wisdom "generously and without reproach" to all who ask Him in prayer. However, in verses 6-8, God also gives direction regarding how we should pray for wisdom. Summarize the main truths found in this text, and explain how we should pray in light of them.

_____

_____

_____

_____

4. The Scriptures abound with promises for those who seek God in prayer to understand His Word and apply it to their lives. Summarize the promises that you find in the following texts, and explain how we should live in light of them.

   a. _Jeremiah 33:3_

   _____

   _____

   _____

   NOTES: Although this promise is given specifically to the prophet Jeremiah, it has a wider application to believers of every age and circumstance. God delights in making known His person, works, and will to those who seek Him by faith.

   b. _Proverbs 2:2-7_

   _____

   _____

_____

_____

_____

c. *Matthew 7:7-11*

_____

_____

_____

_____

_____

5. We have established that prayer is an indispensable element in our interpretation of the Scriptures, but **how** should we pray? Thankfully, we are given an answer! The same Scriptures that admonish us to pray also teach us how to pray. Below, we will consider the prayers of King David and the Apostle Paul. By studying their inspired prayers, we can learn how to ask for God's aid when we are studying His Word. Identify the petitions that are found in each prayer.

a. *Psalm 119:18*

_____

_____

_____

b. *Psalm 119:26-32*

_____

_____

_____

_____

_____

_____

c. *Psalm 119:33-38*

_____

_____

_____

_____

_____

NOTES: Verse 38 could also be translated, "Confirm to your servant your promise, that you may be feared" (ESV).

d. *Ephesians 1:15-19a*

_____

_____

_____

_____

_____

NOTES: There are two possible interpretations for the word "spirit" in verse 17: (1) it is a reference to the Holy Spirit, who is the medium through which God gives wisdom and revelation to His people; or (2) it is a reference to an attitude or disposition in the Christian that allows him to receive and understand the revelation and wisdom that comes from God. Most commentators prefer the former interpretation over the latter.

e. *Colossians 1:9-10*

_____

_____

_____

_____

_____

_____

> **NOTES:** It is important to be reminded that the goal of our study of the Scriptures is not merely the acquisition of knowledge; the ultimate goal is transformation and ability to live in a way that is pleasing to God.

6. We must learn to pray biblically. Based upon the biblical prayers that we studied under Main Point 5, write a prayer to God, asking for aid to study, comprehend, and apply His Word to your life.

_____

_____

_____

_____

_____

_____

_____

_____

Chapter 21: Benefiting from the Word

Part One: Reading and Study

One of the greatest purposes of the Bible is to transform the Christian's character into the likeness of Christ. However, this will be highly improbable if our Bibles are abandoned on the shelf, covered in dust. We must have a daily encounter with the Word of God! In the Bible, we can find at least four methods by which the believer can benefit from God's Word: reading, study, memorization, and meditation. We will dedicate two chapters to these crucial practices.

READ THE WORD

The first step in benefiting from the Word of God is to read it daily. No one would think of studying a literary work without first reading it in its entirety, nor would they think of beginning their reading in the middle of the book or in the last chapter. In the same way, reading through the Bible systematically from Genesis to Revelation is the foundation and first step in our study of the Scriptures.

It is lamentable that there are many Christians who have never read through the entire Bible. Not only are they missing out on a tremendous blessing, but they are also severely limiting their ability to be a blessing to others. Below, we will study the importance of daily and systematically reading through the Bible. It is not just a discipline for the new believer; it should be a practice that the believer faithfully maintains throughout his or her entire life.

1. In Deuteronomy 17:18-20, we clearly see the importance of reading the Word of God. According to this text, what command or responsibility was given to every king of Israel regarding the Scriptures? What does this command teach us, and how should we apply it to our lives?

   _____

   _____

   _____

   _____

   _____

2. We learned from Deuteronomy 17:18-20 that the king of Israel was commanded to read the Law of God "all the days of his life." According to this text, what will we gain from reading the Word of God?

   a. *We learn to F_____ or reverence the Lord (v.19).*

b. *We learn to carefully O_____ the Word of God (v.19).*

c. *We keep our hearts from being L_____ U_____ (v.20).*

> **NOTES:** Reverence, obedience, and humility are foundational virtues of the Christian faith. These can be obtained through a lifetime of faithful reading through the Word of God. We begin in Genesis and finish in Revelation. Then we begin again. By the end of our lives, we should have read through the Scriptures countless times.

3. In I Timothy 4:13, what did the Apostle Paul exhort his young disciple Timothy to do so that he and the local church might grow in their knowledge of the Word?

_____

_____

_____

_____

> **NOTES:** The public reading of the Scriptures in the local church is not an option to be discarded, but a command to be obeyed. It should be a central element in the church service. As the Scriptures are being read, we should discipline our minds to listen intently, knowing that there is great blessing in faithfully listening to the Word.

4. According to Apostle Paul in Ephesians 3:3-4, what could be gained by reading through the letter that he had written to the believers in Ephesus?

a. *They could U_____ his I_____ into the*

   M_____ of Christ!

5. How could the promise in Ephesians 3:3-4 be applied to all of God's Word? Answer this question in light of what Jesus taught in John 5:39.

_____

_____

_____

_____

NOTES: In varying degrees, all Scripture testifies of Jesus Christ. Through reading the Scriptures, we are able to gain greater insight into the wonderful mystery of His person and work.

6. What does Revelation 1:3 promise to every believer who reads its contents? What else besides reading is required?

_____

_____

_____

_____

NOTES: The key truth taught in Revelation 1:3 can be applied to all of the Scriptures. More than mere reading is required if we are to be blessed by the Word. Our reading must be accompanied by heartfelt obedience. As James declared, "But prove yourselves doers of the word, and not merely hearers who delude themselves" (James 1:22). It is only the "effectual doer" who will be "blessed in what he does" (James 1:25).

STUDY THE WORD

Reading the Bible is important, but there is more that we must do if we hope to receive the full blessing of the Word of God. We must not only read, but we must also study in greater depth the things that we have read. Some Christians wrongly believe that an in-depth study of the Scriptures is only for pastors and theologians, but the Bible itself teaches that it is the responsibility of every believer.

1. What does the Apostle Paul command his young disciple Timothy in II Timothy 2:15? How can this command be applied to every Christian?

_____

_____

_____

_____

_____

NOTES: The command, "Be diligent," comes from the Greek word *spoudázō*, which means, "to make haste, to earnestly strive, to be bent on, to do one's best, or to labor over." The phrase "accurately handling" comes from the Greek word *orthotoméō* [*orthós* = straight + *témnō* = to cut], which literally means, "to cut straight," referring to our great need to both interpret and teach the Word of God with the most accuracy possible.

2. Ezra 7:10 is a powerful example of the threefold relationship that every believer ought to have with the Scriptures. According to this text, Ezra set his heart to do what three things?

   a. *To S_____ the Law of the Lord.* From the Hebrew word *darash*, which is literally translated, "to seek." In our study of the Word of God, we are seeking, as one who seeks great treasure.

   b. *To P_____ the Law of the Lord.* Throughout the Scriptures, we are warned that we must be "doers" of the Word and not merely "hearers" who delude themselves (James 1:22-25; Matthew 7:21).

   c. *To T_____ the Law of the Lord.* It is often said that the Christian who does not share the truth that he receives becomes like a stagnant pool. The Word that flows into us ought to flow out to others.

3. How should the three truths listed above be applied to the life of every believer? How should they be applied to your own life?

   _____

   _____

   _____

   _____

   _____

   _____

4. Many believers are intimidated by study, thinking that it is only for the professional theologian. In Acts 17:11-12, we read of the Apostle Paul's ministry in Berea. What does the text say about the Bereans, and how can we imitate their example?

   _____

   _____

_____

_____

_____

_____

NOTES: The word "examining" comes from the Greek verb **_anakrínō_**, which means, "to examine closely, study thoroughly, scrutinize, investigate, appraise, or try someone judicially." The Bereans were not scribes or priests; they were common people who simply had the desire to understand the Word of God. As such, they are an example to all believers everywhere.

5. According to I Corinthians 2:11-12, what gift has been given to the Church and the individual believer so that we might understand God's Word? How is this an encouragement for us to study?

_____

_____

_____

_____

_____

_____

6. According to John 7:17, what must our attitude or disposition be when we study God's Word? In other words, what is the one requirement that the believer must fulfill in order to understand the Word of God?

_____

_____

_____

_____

7. According to Deuteronomy 5:1, what is the great end or goal of all our learning? How should this truth be applied to our lives?

_____

_____

_____

_____

_____

_____

NOTES: The phrase, "observe them carefully," is literally translated, "observe to do them." We are to learn so that we might do. The goal of study is the transformation of our thinking, attitudes, words, and deeds.

Chapter 22: Benefiting from the Word

Part Two: Memorization and Meditation

In the previous chapter, we considered the importance of reading and studying the Scriptures. In this chapter, we will consider the equally important disciplines of memorization and meditation.

MEMORIZE THE WORD

A Biblical Requirement

As we read and study the Scriptures, certain texts will be of special interest to us. It is a wonderful blessing to memorize these texts as a constant reminder of the truths they contain. This internalization of the Word is necessary if we are to gain the greatest possible fruit from our reading and study. We cannot read the Bible twenty-four hours a day, but we can carry it with us through the discipline of memorization.

1. What did God command in Deuteronomy 6:6-9? How does this command demonstrate the great significance of memorizing the Scriptures?

_____

_____

_____

_____

NOTES: After the Babylonian exile, the Jews sought to obey this command literally. They even tied small boxes of Scripture to their foreheads and arms during their morning prayers. The proper interpretation of this text is that we must guard the Word of God in our hearts through memorization so that it might direct our every activity.

2. According to the following Scriptures, what is the purpose of guarding the Word of God in our hearts through memorization?

    a. *Deuteronomy 30:14*

    _____

    _____

_____

_____

NOTES: Obedience to God's commands begins with guarding His Word in our hearts and having it ready upon our lips.

b. *Psalm 37:31*

_____

_____

_____

_____

c. *Psalm 119:11*

_____

_____

_____

_____

NOTES: If we do the opposite of what is commanded here, the result will be devastating: "Your word I have **not** treasured in my heart, that I **may** sin against You."

d. *Colossians 3:16-17*

_____

_____

_____

_____

_____

> **NOTES:** It is interesting and notable that the results of the indwelling Word in the life of the Christian (Colossians 3:16-17) are almost identical to the results of being indwelt and moved by the Holy Spirit (Ephesians 5:18-20). There is a direct relationship between the saturation of the Word of God in our lives and the fullness of the Spirit. The more we fill our lives with the Word, the more we will experience the life and power of the Spirit.

3. Do you live in obedience to God's commands regarding the memorization of His Word? If you are obedient, explain how you memorize the Scriptures. If you are not obedient, explain what changes you are going to make.

_____

_____

_____

_____

_____

_____

A NEGLECTED DISCIPLINE

The memorization of God's Word is one of the most important yet most neglected disciplines in the Christian life. Many Christians use the excuse that they do not have a good memory or that memorizing Scripture is simply too time-consuming. Such attitudes fail to consider that Scripture memory is not a suggestion; it is a direct command from the Bible. Regardless of our abilities, we can all put forth the same effort to memorize God's Word. Although some believers will be more proficient than others, all will receive a blessing and become more useful servants of Christ. The following practical advice is given to help us reach our goal.

1. **We should always remember that Scripture memory is not a suggestion or an option, but a direct command from the Bible.** We will be judged not for how much Scripture we have memorized, but for how diligent we were in obeying the command.

2. **We should begin by memorizing smaller portions of Scripture, such as verses or small paragraphs.** Many Christians give up on Scripture memorization because they attempt to memorize too much material too quickly. Each person should memorize at his or her own pace. The key is consistency, not speed. It is a discipline for the believer's entire life.

3. **We should begin by memorizing the Scriptures that interest us or can help us in our spiritual growth.** For example, if we have a problem with impatience, we should memorize texts that speak to this vice and lead us to the alternative biblical virtue. If we recognize the need to be better witnesses for Christ, we should memorize texts that are helpful in evangelism.

4. **After we have become more consistent in the discipline of memorization, we may recognize the need to memorize Scripture systematically and according to themes.** To accomplish this goal, we simply need to gather those biblical texts that summarize or explain a certain theme and then memorize the texts one by one until we have guarded them in the treasury of our hearts and minds. Before we know it, we will have memorized dozens of Scripture passages relating to the great themes of the Bible. Some possible themes to consider are the gospel, salvation by grace through faith, biblical assurance, the promises of God, or the commands of Scripture—but the list is almost endless!

5. **We should carry our memory verses with us on small cards or a mobile device.** We often waste so much time between our daily activities (waiting for an appointment, taking the bus, mowing the lawn, shaving, cooking, etc.), but we can redeem this time by memorizing Scripture.

6. **Periodically, we should review the Scriptures that we have already memorized so that they stay firmly implanted in our hearts and minds.**

MEDITATE UPON THE WORD

We should not only guard the Word in our hearts, but we should also discipline ourselves to meditate upon it. Many Christians have a wrong view of meditation. When they hear the word, they imagine a guru seated in a lotus position upon a mountain, chanting a mantra. However, meditation is actually a biblical discipline that believers ought to practice.

Biblical meditation is, simply put, the discipline of contemplating the Word of God so that we might understand its truths and that it might have a greater impact on our lives. Consider the way in which cattle eat grass. After chewing and swallowing, the cow then returns the food to its mouth to chew it again. This process is repeated three times, until the cow has received the greatest benefit from the nutrients in the grass. Similarly, in meditation, the Christian simply "chews" on God's Word until the greatest benefit has been gained.

1. In Joshua 1:6-9, God admonishes Joshua to take up the ministry of Moses and to lead the people of Israel into the Promised Land. In this text, we find one of the most powerful admonitions that God has ever given. Read through the text until you are familiar with its contents, and then answer the following questions.

   a. *What was God's command to Joshua in verse 8? How should this same admonition be applied to our own lives?*

   _____

   _____

_____

_____

_____

b. *What were the promised benefits if Joshua obeyed? How can this promise be applied to every believer who takes seriously the command to meditate upon the Word of God?*

_____

_____

_____

_____

2. Psalm 1:1-3 describes the righteous man. Read through the text until you are familiar with its contents, and then answer the following questions.

a. *How is the righteous man described in verses 1 and 2? What is his relationship with the Word of God?*

_____

_____

_____

_____

b. *According to verse 3, what is the result of the righteous man's devotion to God through His Word? How is his life described?*

_____

_____

_____

_____

_____

c. *How does your life compare to that of the righteous man described in Psalm 1:1-3? Are there any changes that ought to be made in your life? Write your thoughts.*

_____

_____

_____

_____

_____

3. King David's love for the Word of God is demonstrated throughout the Scriptures. According to the following texts, what role did meditation have in David's relationship with God and His Word? How should we seek to imitate David?

a. *Psalm 119:15-16*

_____

_____

_____

_____

_____

b. *Psalm 119:147-148*

_____

_____

_____

_____

_____

Chapter 23: Obeying the Scriptures

Reading, studying, memorizing, and meditating upon the Scriptures all have one great purpose—devotion to God manifested in **obedience**. The goal of the Christian life is not just knowledge or understanding; the true aim is the transformation of our characters into the image of Jesus Christ, who lived in perfect obedience to the will of God. Like Him, we must seek to submit our entire lives to God's commands. Only then will we have fulfilled the purpose of the Scriptures for our lives. It is impossible to overemphasize this truth! Our flesh has a tendency to seek knowledge that puffs up and to avoid practical application that requires our submission and obedience. Nevertheless, we must resist this tendency and obey the will of God, which we learn from our study of the Scriptures.

1. According to Deuteronomy 5:29, what is God's great desire for His people?

_____

_____

_____

_____

_____

NOTES: For the New Testament believer, God has made this desire a reality! He has justified us and freed us from the condemnation of sin. He has regenerated us and given us a new heart that desires to do His will. Finally, He has given us both His Word to guide us and His Spirit to teach and strengthen us. Although sin is still a painful reality for every believer, we have been given the means to overcome it and to live a life marked by joyful obedience.

2. According to Deuteronomy 5:1, what are the three appropriate responses of the believer to the commandments of God?

   a. *To H_____ them.* The command is from the Hebrew word **shema**. In this context and many others (*e.g.* Deuteronomy 6:4), it is not just a call to hear but to obey what is heard. The phrase, "in your hearing," is literally, "in your ears." God has spoken plainly; the question is, "Do we have ears to hear?" (see Mark 4:9, 23).

   b. *To L_____ them.* A superficial hearing of God's will does not produce obedience. Obedience can and should flow from a profound knowledge of God's will. We should devote ourselves to understanding all that God has revealed about Himself.

c. O_____ them C_____. The phrase is literally, "observe to do them." We are to learn so that we might do. The goal of study is the transformation of our thoughts, attitudes, words, and deeds.

3. Ezra 7:10 is a powerful example of the threefold relationship that every believer ought to have with the Scriptures. We considered this text only a few chapters ago, but it is worth repeating until we learn to do it! According to this text, Ezra set his heart to do what three things?

   a. To S_____ the Law of the Lord. From the Hebrew word **darash**, which is literally translated, "to seek." In our study of the Word of God, we are seeking, as one who seeks for great treasure.

   b. To P_____ the Law of the Lord. Throughout the Scriptures, we are warned that we must be "doers" of the Word and not merely "hearers" who delude themselves (James 1:22-25; Matthew 7:21).

   c. To T_____ the Law of the Lord. It is often said that the Christian who does not share the truth that he receives becomes like a stagnant pool. The Word that flows into us ought to flow out to others.

4. According to the following Scriptures, how should we respond to God's commands?

   a. Deuteronomy 5:32-33

   _____

   _____

   _____

   _____

   b. Joshua 22:5

   _____

   _____

   _____

   _____

   _____

NOTES: Notice the relationship between love for God and obedience to His commands. Neither can exist without the other.

5. Our knowledge of Scripture is not enough to please God. He desires our reverent and joyful obedience! What do the following texts teach us about this truth?

a. *I Samuel 15:22*

_____

_____

_____

_____

b. *Matthew 7:21; Luke 6:46*

_____

_____

_____

_____

NOTES: We are saved by faith alone and not by obedience to Christ's commands. However, the result and proof of our salvation by faith is our growing obedience to God's will.

c. *John 14:15*

_____

_____

_____

d. *James 1:22-25*

6. The obedience that God's Word demands is an eager, wholehearted, and consistent obedience. Delayed or half-hearted obedience is disobedience. What do the following Scriptures teach us about this truth?

a. *Psalm 119:60*

b. *Psalm 119:112*

7. Many falsely believe that the Scriptures are too difficult to understand or that obedience is burdensome and enslaving. Nothing could be further from the truth! What does God's Word teach us regarding this?

   a. *The believer can comprehend and obey the commandments of God.*

      (1) Deuteronomy 30:11-14

      _____

      _____

      _____

      _____

      (2) Micah 6:8

      _____

      _____

      _____

      _____

   b. *The commandments of God are not burdensome to the believer.*

      (1) I John 5:2-3

      _____

      _____

      _____

      (2) Matthew 11:28-30

      _____

      _____

_____

_____

8. God has given us His commands not to enslave us, but to bring us blessing and joy. What do the following Scriptures teach us about this truth?

    a. *Psalm 19:8, 10-11*

    _____

    _____

    _____

    _____

    _____

    b. *Luke 11:27-28*

    _____

    _____

    _____

    _____

    _____

    c. *James 1:25*

    _____

    _____

    _____

    _____

    _____

Chapter 24: Interpreting the Scriptures

Our interpretation of the Bible determines our beliefs and directs the entire course of our lives. Therefore, we must learn to interpret the Scriptures correctly. In this chapter, we will consider the basic principles of Bible interpretation.

A DEFINITION OF HERMENEUTICS

In the preceding chapters, we have learned about the origins of the Scriptures and their significance for our lives. In this chapter, we will learn about how to study the Bible for ourselves.

When God revealed Himself to men, He chose to do so through a book that employs words, phrases, and rules of language or grammar. Therefore, in order to study the Bible correctly, it is necessary to consider each book in its historical and grammatical context. Furthermore, we must concern ourselves with the original intent of the author, the meaning of words, and the structure and relationship of phrases and paragraphs.

The Bible is a spiritual book and can only be properly interpreted through the illuminating work of the Holy Spirit. The Bible is also a real book, and the only correct interpretation is that which is according to the written grammar. For this reason, it is necessary to study the discipline known as "hermeneutics."

Hermeneutics (Greek: ***hermēneúō*** = to interpret) is the study of Bible interpretation. There are certain rules or principles of interpretation that should be employed in order to study the Bible correctly. Hermeneutics is the study of these principles.

GUIDING PRINCIPLES OF HERMENEUTICS

Hermeneutics, the science of Bible interpretation, is a serious matter. Our interpretation of the Bible determines our beliefs about reality, and these beliefs determine our thoughts and actions. The following is a list of fourteen of the most basic principles of hermeneutics.

1. **The Bible is the highest and only infallible authority for the Christian life.** It is impossible to interpret the Bible correctly unless we believe that it is the infallible Word of God. Otherwise, we will be prone to accept only that which conforms to our view and reject the rest as non-authoritative. When we hold to the infallibility of the entire Bible, we realize that we have no right to reject certain biblical teachings simply because they oppose our culture, traditions, opinions, personal preferences, or lifestyle. We realize that every idea, attitude, and action must be compared to and judged by the Scriptures.

2. **The Bible is sufficient.** We must believe that the Scriptures are sufficient to bring us to a saving knowledge of Christ and to equip the Church and the individual Christian for every good work. Everything that we need for faith and practice is found in the Scriptures. All secular knowledge that claims to bring healing to the heart and mind must be judged by the infallible rule of Scripture (II Timothy 3:15-17).

3. **The Holy Spirit is absolutely necessary in the interpretation of the Scriptures.** Apart from the Spirit's illumination, it is impossible to understand the Bible (I Corinthians 2:14). Therefore, we must study the Scriptures with an attitude of prayer, dependence, and submission. The Holy Spirit is our Teacher; still, this does not mean that in the name of the Spirit we can depart from or add to what is written in God's Word. The Holy Spirit teaches us through the Scriptures, in perfect agreement with what is written. If our personal interpretation contradicts the Bible, it is not a work of the Spirit. Only what is written in the Scriptures should be affirmed as doctrine. Feelings, intuitions, and emotions have no value in the formation of a biblical faith.

4. **The Bible is the best commentary on itself.** The Bible interprets itself. When we cannot understand a text or when we desire to deepen our understanding of a text, we should look for an explanation in other biblical texts. For example, Mark 16:15 commands us to preach the gospel, but I Corinthians 15:1-4 gives a clear definition of the gospel that we are supposed to preach. Or again, Romans 5:1 teaches that we are justified by faith, but Romans 4:6-8 explains the meaning of justification, while Hebrews 11:1 defines genuine faith. Even though tools such as study Bibles and commentaries are very useful in the study of the Scriptures, we should develop the habit of searching the Bible itself for answers to our questions.

5. **The Bible does not contradict itself.** Our interpretations of individual texts or verses should therefore always be in harmony with one another. If our interpretation of one text contradicts our interpretation of another, then we are mistaken. This truth demonstrates the importance of having a general knowledge of all books and doctrines of the Scriptures. For example, we should not interpret the declaration, "God is love" (I John 4:8), as a denial of the justice or wrath of God—the Bible also teaches that God is just (Psalm 119:137) and that His wrath is against those who practice iniquity (Psalm 34:16; Ephesians 5:6).

6. **Texts of Scripture with obscure meanings should be interpreted in light of texts with clear meanings.** For example, in John 14:28, Jesus declared, "The Father is greater than I." Some cults have used this declaration to teach that Jesus is not God in the flesh. However, Christ's statement must be interpreted in light of the many texts that declare His deity (John 1:1, 14, 18; 20:28; Romans 9:5; Philippians 2:6; Colossians 1:15; 2:9; Titus 2:13; Hebrews 1:8) and explain His incarnation. In Philippians 2:6-7, Paul writes, "Although He existed in the form of God, [He] did not regard equality with God a thing to be grasped, but emptied Himself, taking the form of a bond-servant, and being made in the likeness of men." When we harmonize these texts, we understand that Christ was not denying His deity, but simply explaining the nature of His incarnation. Though He is God in the fullest sense of the term, He submitted Himself to the Father in perfect obedience so that He might die for the human race that He came to represent. Another example is found in Hebrews 6:4-8. At first glance, it may appear that the passage is teaching that a genuine believer can lose his salvation and perish forever. However, upon studying this text in the context of the entire book of Hebrews and in light of a multitude of texts that clearly teach the eternal security of the believer, we see that this is not the correct interpretation. Related to this vital principle of hermeneutics is the principle that we should never form a doctrine based upon the supposed meaning of one text whose interpretation is unclear.

7. **Our interpretation should be determined by the grammar (*i.e.* by what is written).** Even though a text of Scripture may have several applications to different believers and circum-

stances, it has only one correct interpretation—the one that agrees with the grammatical meaning. We must first determine what the author intended to say to those to whom he was writing; afterwards, we can deduce abiding truths or principles from the text; finally, we can determine the application to our own lives.

8. **Context is critical.** The word "context" comes from the Latin word ***contextus*** (***con*** = together + ***texere*** = to weave) and refers to all that is related to the text and may influence its interpretation. Scripture is like a puzzle in that we cannot understand the meaning and place of one piece without considering the meaning and place of all the other pieces surrounding it. Many doctrinal errors have occurred because students have interpreted passages of Scripture without considering the following influential factors.

   a. *HISTORICAL CONTEXT* – Who is the author and who are the initial recipients? What is the date in which the book was written? What period of history is being described or narrated? What is the primary purpose of the book? Why was it written and included in the Scriptures?

   b. *GRAMMATICAL CONTEXT* – Truths are expressed in words, which are the building blocks of sentences, which form paragraphs, which unite together in a unified purpose to relate a story or to communicate a truth. We cannot study one text in isolation from the others with which it forms a cohesive narrative, thought, or idea.

   c. *LITERARY CONTEXT* – There are different literary forms in Scripture that will influence the way in which a passage or an entire book might be interpreted. The most basic forms are: history, law, poetry, wisdom, prophecy, parables, and epistles (or letters). Each literary form presents its own interpretive challenges. When studying a historical book, such as Judges, we must learn how to draw universal principles from the text and apply them to contemporary life. When studying a book of the law, such as Leviticus, we must interpret it in light of the coming of Christ, His work on Calvary, and the New Covenant that He has established. When studying prophecies, such as Isaiah, Zechariah, or Revelation, we must discern what is literal and what is figurative.

9. **Words are significant.** God has chosen words to communicate His truth to us. The Bible teaches that "all Scripture is inspired by God" (II Timothy 3:16) and that we are to live "by every word that proceeds out of the mouth of God" (Matthew 4:4). Therefore, it is important that we determine the key words of a text and define them according to their original meaning. Finding the word in a biblical dictionary can be helpful, but we must proceed with great caution. In the Bible, the meaning of a word is significantly influenced by its context; a word may have different meanings in different texts.

10. **The most straightforward interpretation is often the best.** The Bible was not written for lofty theologians or mystics; it was written for the common man. Although there are allegories, metaphors, and symbols, the simplest and most literal interpretation is generally the best. A sound principle to follow is that we should seek a literal interpretation of the text unless a literal interpretation is ridiculous or contradicts the clear meaning of other texts. For example, it would be ridiculous to interpret Psalm 98:8 in literal manner—rivers do not really clap their hands, and mountains do not sing! Similarly, when Jesus declared, "I am the true vine, and My Father is the vinedresser" (John 15:1), He was obviously speaking figuratively.

11. **The Old Testament should be interpreted in light of the New Testament.** The revelation of God's truth in the Bible is progressive. In the Old Testament, the people of God practiced many rituals and sacrifices according to the Law of God that was given to them through Moses. These things were intended to prepare the people for the coming of Christ (Galatians 3:24). They were shadows of a greater reality (Colossians 2:17). With the coming of Christ, these rituals and sacrifices were fulfilled; they should no longer be practiced. The New Testament must be our infallible guide for interpreting and applying the Old Testament to the Christian life.

12. **Our interpretation should not go beyond the revelation given.** Our interpretation should be limited to the information provided in the Scriptures. The Bible contains mysteries that we will never comprehend until we are in heaven (I Corinthians 13:12). What it does not explain should be reverentially treated as a mystery. In other words, we should be silent where the Bible is silent. Furthermore, we should take great care that we do not place demands upon others or ourselves that go beyond the requirements of Scripture. There is a huge difference between a clear truth revealed in the Bible and the inferences, deductions, or speculations that we might make. Deuteronomy 29:29 declares, "The secret things belong to the Lord our God, but the things revealed belong to us and to our sons forever."

13. **The goal is exegesis.** The word "exegesis" comes from the Greek verb **exêgēsis** [**ex** = out + **hēgéomai** = to guide or direct]. To exegete a text means to **draw out** its true meaning rather than to **read into** the text our own presuppositions or ideas. Through our culture, education, and religious upbringing, we have formed ideas of reality that function like filters or colored lenses, influencing and even distorting the way we see things. As students of the Bible, we must recognize this and strive to put aside our presumptions to hear what the Bible is actually saying.

14. **We should study the Scriptures in the context of the Church at large.** Throughout the history of the Church, believers have revered, loved, and studied the Scriptures. At present, there are many pastors, teachers, and theologians who believe that the Bible is the Word of God and study it faithfully. It is wise to compare our personal conclusions to the conclusions of believers living today and of believers throughout history. If all the Bible-believing Christians throughout history are in agreement regarding a certain interpretation of the Bible while our personal interpretation or that of our generation differs with them, it should be a warning to us that we may be in error and should restudy the text.

Appendix: Practical Helps for Reading and Studying Scripture

HELPFUL TOOLS FOR STUDYING GOD'S WORD

Our conviction that the Bible is the best commentary on itself should not restrict us from using other reference tools that are designed to facilitate our study of the Bible. The proper use of dictionaries, concordances, and even commentaries can be of great benefit to the Bible student. As we conclude our study, we will consider a few of the most important reference tools that the Bible student may want to include in his or her library.

ESTABLISHED AND RELIABLE TRANSLATIONS

The use of a few good Bible translations can help us to better understand a text, because they provide us with the opportunity to see the text from different perspectives. A few of the most trustworthy and helpful translations include: the New American Standard Bible (NASB), the King James Version (KJV), the New King James Version (NKJV), the English Standard Version (ESV), and the Christian Standard Bible (CSB).

BIBLE DICTIONARY

A good Bible dictionary is absolutely essential for the Bible student. In the course of our reading and study, we will come across questions regarding terminology, geographical locations, culture, archeology, and more. A good Bible dictionary is an excellent resource for such matters. Some helpful one-volume dictionaries include: *New Bible Dictionary*, *Holman Illustrated Bible Dictionary*, *Harper's Bible Dictionary*, and *Unger's Bible Dictionary*. The *International Standard Bible Encyclopedia* is a sound and affordable multi-volume dictionary.

EXHAUSTIVE CONCORDANCE

An exhaustive concordance provides an alphabetical index of all the words in the Bible and the texts in which they are found. It is similar to the concise concordance that is found at the back of most Bibles, but it is comprehensive in its scope. A concordance is very helpful when doing word studies or when looking for a certain verse without knowing its exact reference. The most widely used concordance is *Strong's Exhaustive Concordance of the Bible*. Keep in mind that it is important to select a concordance that uses the same translation as your Bible.

THEMATIC CONCORDANCE

A thematic concordance orders texts of Scripture by various themes or categories. For example, an exhaustive concordance would not be helpful if a student were searching for all the texts in the Bible that teach about the Trinity, since the word "Trinity" itself is not found in the

Bible. In such a case, the student could turn to a thematic concordance and search the index for the subject "Trinity." There the student would find a list of the prominent texts dealing with that subject. Two of the most helpful thematic concordances are *Nave's Topical Bible* and *Topical Analysis of the Bible: A Survey of Essential Christian Doctrines*.

WORD STUDIES

At times, the student will be required to research the meaning of certain biblical terms. In such a case, it is crucial that the student have access to resources of accurate scholarship. Although word studies are beneficial—even essential—they can lead to error. The same word does not always carry the same meaning in its every occurrence in the Bible; rather, the meaning is determined by the context. If we study a certain word without considering its context in every instance, then we are prone to be led astray. The most helpful one-volume word study aid is *Mounce's Complete Expository Dictionary of Old and New Testament Words*. Two excellent multi-volume sets are the *Theological Wordbook of the Old Testament* and the *New International Dictionary of New Testament Theology*.

STUDY BIBLES

Study Bibles are helpful as a quick and concise reference tool. When the student is reading through the Bible, it is often difficult or cumbersome to pull away in order to research basic questions that might arise (*e.g.* "Who wrote this book, and when?" "Where was Nineveh located?" "What are the most common views regarding Revelation 20?"). A good study Bible is helpful in such instances, because it can provide the student with just enough information to keep reading. However, we must always remember that the only part of a study Bible that is inspired is the Bible itself! Some helpful study Bibles would include: *New American Standard Study Bible, ESV Study Bible, Reformation Study Bible, MacArthur Study Bible,* and *Holman Study Bible*.

COMMENTARIES

Before discussing commentaries, we must understand two significant truths. First, only the Scriptures are inspired and infallible; the very best of scholars and scholarly works cannot make this claim. Secondly, although it is very beneficial to use commentaries, we must not allow them to overshadow our study of the Scriptures.

What then are the benefits of good commentaries? First, they allow us to benefit from a certain author's years of research on a book or text in which the average student may only be able to invest a few hours. Secondly, multiple commentaries on the same book allow us to compare and contrast various perspectives and even interpretations on a certain book or text. Thirdly, commentaries can be used as sounding boards to test or critique our own conclusions. "Dialoguing" with the authors of different commentaries may bring to light error in our own thinking or help us to refine our thoughts about a certain text or doctrine. Two of the most useful one-volume commentaries are the *New Bible Commentary* (InterVarsity Press) and the *Baker Commentary on the Bible. Matthew Henry's Commentary* is one of the most beloved devotional commentaries in the history of the Church. It comes both in a concise one-volume edition and as a multi-volume set. Two of the most useful multi-volume commentaries are the *Expositor's Bible Commentary* and the *Tyndale Commentaries: Old and New Testament*.

A PRACTICAL GUIDE FOR READING GOD'S WORD

One of the most beneficial spiritual disciplines is the daily and systematic reading of the Scriptures. The best way to grow in our knowledge of the Bible is simply to read it from cover to cover, over and over again. In this final chapter, we will consider a few practical suggestions for cultivating the lifelong discipline of reading through the Bible.

1. **Schedule your Bible reading for a specific time each day.** It is difficult to form a new habit in our lives, and the discipline of daily Bible study is no exception. The flesh is weak and hindering to spiritual devotion (Matthew 26:41). Furthermore, the devil will do everything in his power to keep us from the Scriptures, because he knows that they are the great source of the believer's spiritual strength. We must therefore make every effort in the grace and power of God to maintain our daily reading of the Scriptures. Those who do will make tremendous progress in the things of God. Persistence is key!

2. **Seek out a quiet place for Bible study.** We read the Scriptures in order to meet with God and hear His Word. It is the most important hour of the day! Therefore, we should seek out a time and place where there will be limited interruptions or distractions—a place where we can unite our mind and heart in the purpose of knowing God and His will.

3. **Do not hurry.** One of the greatest obstacles to an effective Bible study is hurry. Like Martha, so many things often worry us; nevertheless, like Mary, we must learn to sit at the feet of Christ and hear His Word. As the Lord said, "only one thing is necessary," and we must learn to choose the "good part" (Luke 10:38-42).

4. **Saturate your reading time in prayer.** The Holy Spirit wrote the Bible, and He is its best Teacher. Regardless of our intellectual or literary capacity, we cannot understand the Scriptures apart from His illuminating work. For this reason, we must pray before, during, and after our reading—that God might give us the wisdom and grace not only to understand His Word but also to obey it.

5. **Read the Bible systematically.** One of the best ways to grow in our knowledge of the Bible is to read it systematically from Genesis to Revelation as many times as possible throughout our lives. We must remember that the Bible is a compilation of sixty-six books that can only be correctly understood in the context of their relationship to one another. The more we understand the Bible as a whole, the better we will understand its individual parts. The systematic reading of the Scriptures from cover to cover should be a lifelong discipline of every believer.

6. **Be perseverant and consistent.** It is best to set a goal of reading the same number of chapters every day. If we read five chapters each day, we can read through the entire Bible in less than a year. There will be days when we fail. The most important thing is that we do not become discouraged. No matter how many times we fail, we are not defeated if we persevere!

7. **Record your thoughts.** In Mark 4:24, Jesus said: "Take care what you listen to. By your standard of measure it will be measured to you; and more will be given you besides." We must learn to appreciate everything that the Lord shows us in His Word and do everything within our means to hold on to it! Because of poor stewardship of the truth that we have received, we must often learn the same lessons over and over again.

8. **Keep references handy.** As we read, there will be questions that we cannot answer and texts that we do not understand. For this reason, it is helpful to use a study Bible or to have a one-volume commentary available for quick reference. It is crucial, especially in the first few times that we read through the Scriptures, that we do not get bogged down in what we do not understand. We should remember that each time we read through the Scriptures we will be able to answer more of our own questions, while at the same time different questions will come to mind.

9. **Always keep in mind that the goal is application, transformation, and obedience.** Knowledge without application is useless. When we study the Scriptures, we should ask ourselves the following questions: "How does this apply to my life here and now? How should I live in light of what I have learned? Do I need to change? What must I do to obey?"

10. **Share with others what you have learned.** In Matthew 10:8, Jesus said, "Freely you received, freely give." The Christian who does not share the blessings that he receives from the Lord becomes like a stagnant pond, but the one who shares is like a river of living water.

HeartCry Missionary Society at a Glance:

The HeartCry Missionary Society began in 1988 in the country of Peru with a desire to aid indigenous or native missionaries so that they might reach their own peoples and establish biblical churches among them. Since then, the Lord has expanded our borders to include not only Latin America but also Africa, Asia, Eurasia, Europe, the Middle East, and North America.

The goal of our ministry is to facilitate the advancement of indigenous missionaries throughout the world. Our strategy consists of four primary components: financial support, theological training, Scripture and literature distribution, and the supply of any tool necessary to facilitate the completion of the Great Commission.

We currently support approximately 250 missionary families (along with a number of ongoing projects) in over 40 nations around the globe.

Introduction to HeartCry

HeartCry Missionary Society was founded and still exists for the advancement of four major goals:

• The Glory of God
• The Benefit of Man
• The Establishment of Biblical Churches
• The Demonstration of God's Faithfulness

1. The Glory of God

Our first major goal is the glory of God. Our greatest concern is that His Name be great among the nations from the rising to the setting of the sun (Malachi 1:11) and that the Lamb who was slain might receive the full reward for His sufferings (Revelation 7:9-10). We find our great purpose and motivation not in man or his needs but in God Himself; in His commitment to His own glory; and in our God-given desire to see Him worshiped in every nation, tribe, people, and language. We find our great confidence not in the Church's ability to fulfill the Great Commission, but in God's unlimited and unhindered power to accomplish all He has decreed.

2. The Benefit of Man

Our second major goal is the salvation of a lost and dying humanity. The Christian who is truly passionate about the glory of God and confident in His sovereignty will not be unmoved by the billions of people in the world who have "had no news" of the gospel of Jesus Christ (Romans 15:21). If we are truly Christ-like, the lost multitude of humanity will move us to compassion (Matthew 9:36), even to great sorrow and unceasing grief (Romans 9:2). The sincerity of our Christian confession should be questioned if we are not willing to do all within our means to make Christ known among the nations and to endure all things for the sake of God's elect (II Timothy 2:10).

3. The Establishment of Local Churches

Our third major goal is the establishment of biblical churches. While we recognize that the needs of mankind are many and his sufferings are diverse, we believe that they all spring from a common origin: the radical depravity of his heart, his enmity toward God, and his rejection of truth. Therefore, we believe that the greatest possible benefit to mankind comes through the preaching of the gospel and the establishment of local churches that proclaim the full counsel of God's Word and minister according to its commands, precepts, and wisdom. Such a work cannot be accomplished through the arm of the flesh, but only through the supernatural providence of God and the means which He has ordained: biblical preaching, intercessory prayer, sacrificial service, unconditional love, and true Christ-likeness.

4. The Demonstration of God's Faithfulness

The fourth and final goal at HeartCry is to demonstrate to God's people that He is truly able and willing to supply all our needs according to His riches in glory. The needs of this ministry will be obtained through prayer. We will not raise support through self-promotion, prodding, or manipulating our brothers and sisters in Christ. If this ministry is of the Lord, then He will be our Patron. If He is with us, He will direct His people to give, and we will prosper. If He is not with us, we will not and should not succeed. Admittedly, our faith has always been meager and frail throughout the years; but God has always been faithful. As one dear brother puts it: our God delights in vindicating even the smallest confidence of His children.

The Challenge

As Christians, we are called, commissioned, and commanded to lay down our lives so that the gospel might be preached to every creature under heaven. Second only to loving God, this is to be our magnificent obsession. There is no nobler task for which we may give our lives than promoting the glory of God in the redemption of men through the preaching of the gospel of Jesus Christ. If the Christian is truly obedient to the Great Commission, he will give his life either to go down into the mine or to hold the rope for those who go down (William Carey). Either way, the same radical commitment is required.

For more information:

Visit our website at **heartcrymissionary.com** for more information about the ministry—our purpose, beliefs, and methodologies—and extensive information about the missionaries we are privileged to serve.

Printed in Great Britain
by Amazon